INTRODUCTION TO
GEOGRAPHY

DANTES/DSST* Test Study Guide

© 2020 Breely Crush Publishing, LLC

*DSST is a registered trademark of Prometric and its affiliated companies, and does not endorse this book.

971050220143

Published by Breely Crush Publishing, LLC
10808 River Front Parkway
South Jordan, UT 84095
www.breelycrushpublishing.com

ISBN-10: 1-61433-744-6
ISBN-13: 978-1-61433-744-7

Printed and bound in the United States of America.

*DSST is a registered trademark of Prometric and its affiliated companies, and does not endorse this book.

 Table of Contents

 *Introduction to Geography*

On the broadest level, geography is the study of land or landscapes and how people interact with them. In the literal sense, the term geography originates from the Greek "geo" which refers to the earth, and "graphy" referred to writings or drawings. The encompasses a wide variety of topics from cultural aspects of how a populations location will affect their beliefs and practices, all the way to political factors such as borders, economic systems, and others. In addition to culture and politics, geography additionally considers factors such as nature, space, and population. Geographers do this in terms of specific locations such as cities or states, and they do it in global contexts. What it all comes down to is that geography attempts to explain human actions as they are caused by, relate to, and affect one thing – location.

In geography, the world can be represented in a number of different ways. The two most common methods used to represent the world are using a globe and using a flat map. Each of these methods is associated with different positive and negative aspects. Globes are useful because they are the most accurate representations of the actual surface of the earth. Because the earth is a sphere, the globe can show the relationships between different landmasses, oceans, and features most accurately.

However, globes can be disadvantageous because they are small-scale and therefore not always the most useful representations. Also, because they are round it is impossible to get a whole-earth view at once, so studying large distances can be difficult.

Maps

In contrast, flat maps are very easy to use in judging distances, and are far more portable than globes are. However, it is important to keep in mind when examining a flat map that there will be distortions in the representation of different factors because of the conversion from three dimensions to two.

Distance plays an important part in this study. People identify and create regions, and, regions encourage people's activities. When regions are developed through agriculture or industry, lands or industry situated far away from human habitations demand less rent. Locations are known by longitude and latitude, a distance that can isolate locations. Locations can be in different directions; map reading is an integral part of learning geography. Direction is normally shown:

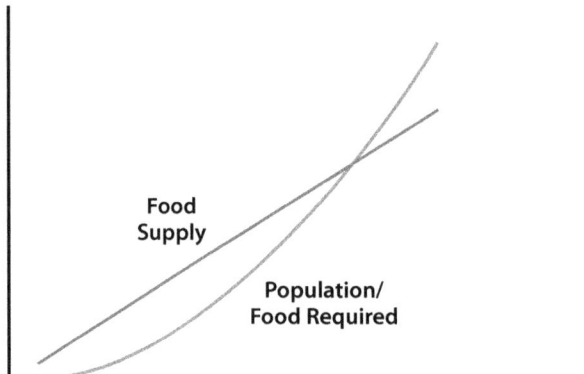

N
V ◁ ◯ ▷ E
S

North
East
West
South

NEWS!

When contour lines on a map take the shape of a "V" this can indicate two different things. If the point of the lines is directed "downhill" in terms of elevation, this indicates a ridge. On the other hand, if the point of the V is directed "uphill" this is an indication of a valley. Usually these coincide with nearby bodies of what that drain down through an area, causing a depression in the elevation over time.

Important to understanding the relative distance shown on a map or globe is the map key. This information is usually included at the bottom of the map and provides the means of calculating the distance between cities or counties.

Other information that is important to know is the chart found below:

Food
Supply

Population/
Food Required

Inch to...	Ratio
Foot	1:12
Yard	1:36
Mile	1:63,360
Meter	1: 39
Kilometer	1:39,370

Latitude and Longitude

The most prominent and common lines to be found on maps are lines of latitude and longitude. Therefore, understanding these two types of lines is extremely important in geography. First, lines of latitude are the horizontal running lines that circle the earth. The most well-known line of latitude is the equator, which runs about the center of the earth at its widest point.

Latitude lines are used to describe absolute location north or south of the equator. Often, these lines are referred to as parallels. Because the earth is a giant sphere, latitude (and longitude) is measured in terms of degrees. Moving from the equator, latitude can be anywhere from zero to ninety degrees north (for the northern hemisphere), or zero to ninety degrees south (for the southern hemisphere. With the equator representing zero degrees. On the globe, each degree represents an approximately 69 mile distance.

Secondly, lines of longitude are the vertical running lines that circle the earth. Lines of longitude are often referred to as meridian lines.

Prime Meridian

The central or "zero degree" meridian line is referred to as the Prime Meridian. Throughout history there has been much debate about where the Prime Meridian should lie; however, today it is accepted that the Prime Meridian runs through Greenwich, the site of the British Royal Observatory.

In contrast to lines of latitude which range from zero to ninety degrees, lines of longitude run from zero to one hundred and eighty degrees east or west (moving outward from Greenwhich) and meet at the international date line in the middle of the Pacific Ocean (on the opposite side of the world as the Prime Meridian).

Isotherm Lines

In some cases it is helpful to know the relationship of temperatures in different areas of the world, or in different parts of a specific region. Lines on a map which outline points of equal temperatures are referred to as isotherm lines. Isotherm originates from "iso" for same and "therm" for temperature. Often times when these lines are seen on a map they will appear as contour lines outlining different regions which are highlighted in different colors to show the temperature breakdowns. Isothermal maps can be created for a specific point in time, or in reference to average temperatures in an area.

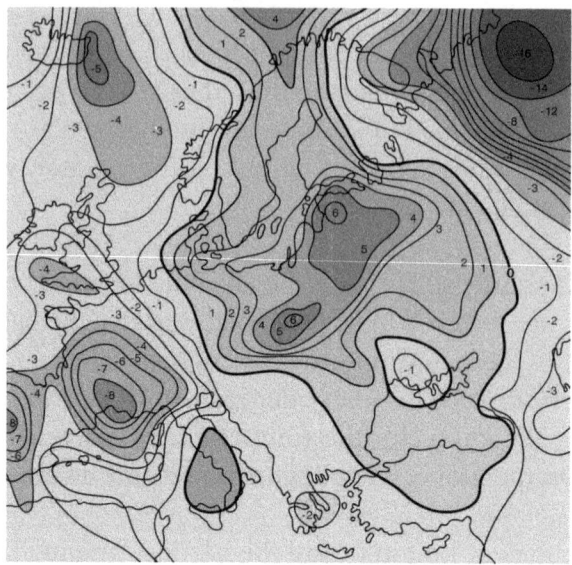

🎓 Biomes

The earth can be divided into biomes which are used to characterize the geography, climate, and diversity of life when exist in a particular area. The nine important biomes to be familiar with are taigas, grasslands, deciduous forests, tropical rainforests, deserts, tundras, alpines, and savannas.

🎓 Taiga

The taiga is the largest biome in the world. Taiga is the Russian word for forest, which typifies this biome. The taiga biome is characterized by very cold, high-elevation, evergreen forests. Food availability is inconsistent and many animals simply hibernate or leave during winters. Many are large, predatory creatures. The taiga biome spans a majority of Russia and Canada.

Grasslands

Grasslands are a bit harder to classify than taigas. Basically, a grassland is any area which receives enough rain for grass to grow and thrive, but not enough to adequately support any other type of vegetation. Although grasslands receive rain sufficient for grass to grow, because they are still fairly hot and dry, they are also characterized by fires which periodically wipe out any type of vegetation which may have begun growing. Grasslands are typically located in the northern temperate climate regions (between the Tropic of Cancer and the Arctic Circle).

They are also typically located inland. The majority of grasslands are found either in inland North America, where they are known as prairies or meadows, or in central Eurasia (including Russia through Northern Africa, Turkey and parts of India). Other names by which grasslands are known include steppes (such as in Russia), fields, pampas (in South America), pastures, and plateaus. Although grasslands are characterized by grass as the primary vegetation, they can still support diverse wildlife populations and vegetation.

Deciduous Forest

In the deciduous forest biome the primary type of vegetation are deciduous trees. Most simply defined, deciduous trees are trees that lose their leaves in the winter. Because of the density of the tree populations, deciduous forests will often not have a variety of vegetation outside trees, but the trees themselves can be quite diverse. Many will be flowering, have different types of fruit, and have a variety of bark and wood types. The trees provide a food source and home space for the variety of animals that inhabit the biome.

Most deciduous forests are located in the Northern temperate climate zones, primarily in the western United States, Eastern China, and Europe. They rotate through four seasons and have an average temperature around 50 degrees Fahrenheit. Because they can have harsher winters, many of the animals which thrive in deciduous forests either migrate or hibernate in the winter months. For example, bears, birds, foxes, and raccoons are all common to deciduous forests.

 # Tropical Rainforest

The next biome is the tropical rainforest. The two words which best describe this biome are warm and wet. Tropical rain forests are located in the tropics (i.e., around the equator spreading as far as the Tropic of Cancer and the Tropic of Capricorn). There are three primary rainforests on earth: the American Rainforest also known as the Amazon Rainforest in Brazil, the African Rainforest, spreading outward near Congo, and the Asian Rainforest, which occupies all of Southeastern Asia. Although rainforests are not the largest biome in terms of spatial area (occupying only 6 percent of the Earth's surface) they support an immense diversity of plants and animals – over half of the species on earth exist in rainforests.

Rainforests are characterized primarily by massive trees and their huge diversity of birds, animals, and especially insects. Various species of monkeys and apes are a characteristic animal of rainforests. The trees are typically quite tall, reaching 250 feet, and usually not branching off until at least 100 or more feet off of the ground. In places where the canopy of trees does open up to allow sunlight through there is also a healthy population of shrubberies.

 # Desert

The next biome is the desert biome. Technically, deserts either can be hot and dry or they can be cold. In this case cold deserts are considered a separate biome – the tundra. A hot and dry desert is the typically desert that comes to mind – the Atacama, Mojave, Namib, Gobi, Sahara and Australian deserts for example. They are characterized by very sparse vegetation, if any. The primary feature of such deserts is sand. Hot and dry deserts are typically located near the Tropics of Capricorn and Cancer.

This is because they are near enough to the equator to receive copious amounts of hot, directly sunlight; however, at the same time they are far enough from the equator to experience the dry air and winds that are more characteristic of the temperate climates (hence the combination of hot and dry characteristics). Hot and dry deserts receive very little, concentrated amounts of rainfall. Because of this, plant and animal species must be expertly adapted to store and find water.

Many different types of deserts exist, and they come in all different forms. Some deserts, for example, are characterized by the frigid temperatures and low rainfall of polar regions. Other deserts are characterized by the presence of tall, tropical mountains which block rain from reaching the area. One common form of desert is the coastal or west coast desert. These deserts are so named because they occur in coastal areas, typically on the west coast of regions located around the tropics of cancer and Capricorn. These deserts are fairly complex, and occur as a result of trade winds that run parallel to the coast, rather than pulling in the rainfall. West coast deserts are less stable than other forms of deserts, and are characterized by occasional heavy fogs that pull in off of the ocean and shadow the area (without bringing any actual rainfall).

One excellent example of a west coast desert is the Atacama Desert. This desert lies on the western coast of South America, primarily in Chile. The Atacama Desert is the driest place on earth, receiving as little as 1 mm of rain every 5-20 years. Other examples of west coast deserts include the Namib Desert, located along Africa's western coast near the tropic of Capricorn, and the Great Sandy Desert, located along Australia's Northwestern coast.

Tundras

In contrast, cold deserts or tundras are found in the Arctic/Antarctic circles of the world. Tundras receive lots of snow in the winters, and rain through the summers. Similarly to deserts, tundras are characterized by sparse vegetation; however, rather than as a result of little rainfall, in tundras the sparse vegetation is a result of cold conditions and snow cover for a large portion of the year. It is important to note, though, that tundras do not have glacial snow and ice year-round. Rather, in a tundra the temperature is near freezing during the winter, and yet reaches near 60 degrees Fahrenheit in the summers.

The world's tundras are primarily found in ring around the North Pole (i.e., along the Arctic Circle). Because of the harsh conditions in tundras, there is also a lower diversity of animal life. Though there are animals native to tundra regions, they are primarily smaller, burrowing animals, like rabbits, that can dig down in the snow for warmth.

Alpines

Alpines are the next biome. The alpine regions derive their name from the Latin term for mountain – alpes. As a result, the alpine biome isn't found in a particular region of the world, but is rather characteristic of a particular altitude. The three primary alpine regions in the world are the Sierra and Rocky Mountains running throughout the Eastern US, the Andes of Chile, and the Alps in Asia. Essentially an alpine recreates the conditions in a taiga. Alpines fall just below the snow line on the mountain, so while they are not glacial, they are quite cold.

Alpines are also characterized by coniferous trees in the lower parts, and smaller lichens and grasses in the higher parts. Alpines tend to be windy and get little rainfall (remember, they are similar to taigas but in mountains). As a result, the soil is rocky and not good for growing. The animal life is also not particular diverse in Alpine biomes. Animals must have large lungs because of the lower levels of oxygen in the air, and thick skin to protect then for the cold. Animals found in this area include several bird species, mountain goats, and squirrels.

Savanna

The final biome is the savanna. Savannas essentially serve as the transition area between deserts and tropical rainforests. For this reason they are also known as tropical grasslands. This is essentially what a savanna is. Savannas are characterized by a warm temperature year round. They are essentially rolling grasslands, with an added diversity of trees and shrubberies in addition to the grasses and low hugging plants. The primary area where savannas are found is in Africa, the southern tip of India and Northern Australia. The animals found in savannas are primarily large herbivores and the carnivores that hunt them. For example, giraffes, lines, tigers, zebras, elephants, and many other animals are found in savannas.

Climate

One of the most important factors in determining the general climate of an area is latitude, or how far north or south of the equator a country is. Latitude is such an important factor for two reasons. First, the areas of the world that lie nearest to the equator receive the greatest amount of sunlight. They are closer to the sun and get more hours of daylight per day. In fact, some polar regions may receive only an hour or so of sun exposure at certain points of the year. Latitude is also important because it affects how direct the sunlight is. The equator receives the most direct sunlight, in addition to simply the most sunlight. The more direct sunlight is, the warmer a climate will be. Areas farther from the equator receive less direct sunlight (because the surface of the earth is round), so even during the hours of daylight they do not receive the same levels of heat.

There are five major latitude lines that roughly divide the world into areas with different climates. Of course specific regions can and do have unique features that may allow them to deviate from specific patterns, in general the three types of world areas are the tropics, the temperate zones, and the arctic.

Tropic Zones

The tropic zones are those which lie between the Tropic of Cancer and the Tropic of Capricorn. The Tropic of Cancer is located at approximately 25 degrees north of the equator. This means that it runs through Hawaii, Mexico, Egypt, India, and the areas with this same approximate latitude. What is unique about the Tropic of Cancer is that it is northernmost point on the earth that is considered to receive direct sunlight. It's counterpart, the Tropic of Capricorn, is the southernmost point on the earth that is considered to receive direct sunlight.

The Tropic of Capricorn is located at approximately 25 degrees south of the equator. This means that it runs through Australia, the southern tip of Africa, and the very northern part of Argentina. Notice that the area between these two tropics is the "tropical" areas of the world. These places are consistently warm and have more stable climates than other areas. They make popular vacation spots and are often more populous than more extreme, polar regions.

Temperate Zones

The temperate zones are the zones which lie between the two tropics and the major latitude lines known as the Arctic Circle and the Antarctic Circle. The Arctic Circle is located at approximately 65 degrees north of the equator. This means that it passes through Greenland, and the most northern parts of Russia and Canada. Because it is north of the equator, the area between the Tropic of Cancer and the Arctic Circle (i.e., approximately 30-60 degrees north latitude) is called the Northern Temperate Zone.

This zone encompasses the majority of the United States, Europe, and China. It's counterpart, the Southern Temperate Zone is bounded by the Tropic of Capricorn and the Antarctic Circle. The Antarctic circle is located at approximately 65 degrees south of the equator, meaning that it just brushes the tip of South America. As a result, the Southern Temperate Zone encompasses the southern portion of South America, Australia, and Southern Africa. In the temperate zones, the sun is never directly overhead (i.e., they do not receive directly sunlight), however they do receive a reasonable amount of sunlight each day. As a result, the climate is considered temperate or mild. These areas are characterized by having four seasons that they cycle through annually.

Arctic Zones

The arctic zones are the polar areas encompassed by the Arctic Circle to the north, and the Antarctic Circle to the south. These areas are frigid, and receive both inconsistent and indirect sunlight. For instance, the North Pole receives a whole 24 hours of sunlight on the summer solstice, but receives absolutely no sunlight on the winter solstice. These areas are characterized by rugged terrain that is often uninhabitable.

Climate is also determined by whether an area is north or south of the equator. In general, areas north of the equator have their summer around July and their winter around January. In contrast, areas south of the equator have their summer around January and their winter around July. These annual cycles are most notable in the temperate zones which are characterized by having seasons, but are also visible to a lesser degree in tropical zones.

Aridisol

Aridisol is a term used by the United States in classifying soils. The term aridisol is used to describe soils which are arid, dry, and not suitable for the growth of vegetation. Often aridisols occur in colder areas, so in addition to the fact that very little grows near them, the decomposition process is quite slow. As a result, aridisols are primarily found in desert areas. Aridisols occupy about 10 percent of the soils in the United States alone, and constitute one-third of the earth's surface (although much of this 33 percent is covered in ice). Aridisols are found primarily in the western part of the United States, in the states of Arizona, Utah, New Mexico, Nevada, Colorado and Wyoming.

Hydrologic Cycle

Water continually circulates at the surface of the earth. It evaporates from oceans into the atmosphere. As clouds, it drifts over land where it condenses and falls as rain or snow. Then it runs off the continents as rivers and streams or it soaks through the soil and rocks. Eventually it reaches the ocean again. The water that soaks into the earth can be drawn up into plants where it evaporates from the leaves and goes back into the atmosphere. The water in the rivers and lakes has some evaporation as well. The whole process is called the water cycle or hydrologic cycle.

Water that falls to Earth in the form of rain, snow, sleet, and hail is called precipitation. Precipitation is part of a continuous process in which water at the Earth's surface evaporates, condenses into clouds, and returns to Earth. This process is termed the water cycle. The water located below the surface is called groundwater.

The impacts of altitude upon climatic conditions are primarily related to temperature and precipitation. As altitude increases, climatic conditions become increasingly drier and colder. Solar radiation becomes more severe as altitude increases while the effects of convection forces are minimized. Climatic changes as a function of latitude follow a similar pattern (as a reference, latitude increases as you move either north or south from the equator). The climate becomes colder and drier as the distance from the equator increases. Proximity to land or water masses produces climatic conditions based upon the available moisture. Dry and arid climates prevail where moisture is scarce; lush tropical climates can prevail where moisture is abundant. Climate, as described above, depends upon the specific combination of conditions making up an area's environment. Man impacts all environments by producing pollutants in earth, air, and water.

Rain Shadow

Rain shadow is a climate phenomenon that typically occurs in areas where there is a large mountain range located near an ocean. What happens is that storms move into the area off of the ocean; however, as they move inward the air is pulled up the side of the mountain and due to changing altitude becomes cooler and drier. As a result, the far or downwind or leeward side of the mountain is essentially blocked from receiving moisture and a desert is created. This is referred to as rain shadow. Some prominent examples of rain shadow include the Gobi Desert, a rain shadow of the Himalayas; Death Valley, a rain shadow of the Sierra-Nevada in California; and the Atacama Desert, a rain shadow of the Andes.

Streams and Rivers

Rivers pass through three stages – youth, maturity, and old age. Each river is different. Some pass through the stages very slowly over thousands of years. Some seem to skip a stage. Others pass through one stage quickly and get stuck in another for hundreds of years. Even in the course of going through a stage, the river will change character as it wears away mountains or builds up plains or delta.

Most rivers begin in mountainous regions. Rain and melting snow causes heavy runoff on the steep slopes. The land which is drained by a river or stream is called its watershed or drainage basin. The runoff cuts small channels in the earth as it flows. Channels join together to form larger channels. And the channels begin to cut into the earth and to pick up small rocks and debris. The larger channels join to form streams which join to form a river. The channels to streams and streams to river pattern appears like the branches and trunk of a tree, so are called a dendritic drainage pattern. More and more rocks, soil and debris are swept away with the water.

A radial drainage pattern occurs when streams flow outward in several directions from an upland area. This can be seen on a volcano or where there is a dome of sedimentary rock such as beds that have heaved up over a laccolith. If the original rock eventually erodes, the rivers continue on the courses they have used since they were young. This lack of respect for the underlying geology is known as superimposed drainage.

Sometimes the strata are composed of hard rock interbedded with softer rock such as layers of sandstone and shale. The soft rock erodes first. The river follows the outcrop of the softer rock and flows parallel to it. As a result, a trellised drainage pattern occurs with the streams following the grain of the landscape (called the strike). They are connected by main streams running at right angles to them.

Sometimes the headwaters (beginning of the stream) will erode back, meeting up with another stream. When this occurs, one will abandon its original channel and combine with the other, forming a river capture.

During the youthful stage, the river is constantly eroding rocks, allowing exposures and cross-sections to be seen. It is full of splash and vigor, forming waterfalls and rapids. A youthful river can drop quite steeply over a short distance. The force and speed of the water forms deep gullies. Much rocky debris can be picked up and carried by the strong current. This causes the river to often be muddy.

A young river wears away bedrock and exposes fossils. It creates a steep-sided V-shaped valley. It can cut deeply into and through many layers of rock during this stage, forming a deep, steep canyon. The immature, or young, river covers almost the entire valley floor. Because of the force of the water, large pieces of rock as well as smaller rock and masses of sediment can be carried many miles by a young river.

As a river matures, rock at the upper side of a waterfall or rapid becomes eroded. The rock being carried by the river creates abrasion on the rock of the riverbed, smoothing all the rock involved and taking off all the edges. The amount of drop lessens. And the riverbed widens. Spring flooding occurs, widening the valley. Trees may be washed downriver during flooding. Those trees may have rocks intertwined in their roots. The area around the river becomes broader and flatter. The river becomes more curved and winding and forms loops called meanders. The flow of water slows down, so the erosion slows down.

Material is still removed at the outside of each curve and deposited on the inside of the curve, but the size particles are smaller and the distance of travel is much less. Deposited debris is more evident than bedrock. Wherever there is slowing, there is more deposition than erosion. The bluffs of the valley may be cut down to the native rock, but they may be overgrown with brush and trees.

With further aging, the landscape around the river becomes more and more worn down. It has made a progression from mountainous to rolling to gently rolling to basically flat. Eventually it becomes a peneplain, meaning "almost a plain." Peneplains usually are not much above sea level. Hills of rock that have resisted weathering and erosion on the peneplain are called monadnocks.

There are times when a mature river is in an area that is uplifted. The river will again cut down into its bed. The result is a gorge that meanders called an incised meander. The best known example is the Brahmaputra River which starts in China, cuts south through the Himalayas to India and then through Bangladesh to the Indian Ocean. It appears to have drained the Asian continent before the Himalayas were uplifted by a tectonic plate collision. This is a phenomenal example of superimposed drainage.

A river that is in old age is weak and slow-moving. It seldom causes erosion of rock, but continues to carry soil and sediment and deposit it. When flooding occurs, debris and sediment is deposited throughout the valley. Banks called levees develop. Loops and islands are formed as part of the river bypasses a meander. Rivers moving down out of mountains or hills typically do so in a straight fashion; however, once they reach flatter ground they have a tendency to meander back and forth in random curved patterns. This generates a process of erosion and subduction at the curving points of the river. Minerals will be deposited and build up on the inside of the curve, and the water will further erode the outside of the curve. When a river meanders in a loop or horseshoe shape, therefore, eventually the erosion process will cut through the center so that the river no longer goes all the way around, but goes straight through and cuts off the outer loop. The resulting independent body of water is referred to as an oxbow lake, due the curved shape that it will have.

On both sides of a mature river or stream are flat areas called floodplains. Because that is the area of overflow during flooding, the river deposits rich sediment (alluvium) and soil in floodplains. As a result of repeated flooding, the soil of floodplains is rich and fertile. This makes them rich farming areas, but areas that are subject to being washed out in the event of heavy rains – even if the rains are upstream. If there is frequent flooding, marshes and water meadows may result. Marshes are wet grasslands; swamps are waterlogged forests.

Where a river flows into the ocean is its mouth. The river's speed decreases as it flows into a lake or ocean, so the river gets wider. Both the slower speed and the increased width cause the river to dump large amounts of the sediment it is carrying. This forms a delta. Deltas can be very large as in the case of the Mississippi River delta. In such a case, the coastal area is increased by hundreds of square kilometers.

As the river's fresh water becomes mixed with the ocean's salt water, salt marshes often develop. An estuary is an area formed at the mouth of a river where river currents interact with ocean tides. Estuaries are rich habitats for many living organisms and animals. One type of estuary (example: the Chesapeake Bay) is formed when seawater swamps the river because the ocean level rises. Another type (example: Waddansee estuary in the Netherlands) is formed when the continuous action of waves builds sand up across the mouth of a river and traps river water behind it. A third type, the fjord seen in Norway and Alaska, forms when rivers end in deep areas of water that are partially isolated from the sea. And finally, earthquakes and volcanoes create a low-lying estruary area in a coastline with only a narrow opening to the sea such as is seen with the San Francisco Bay.

The Nile River in Africa is the longest river in the world at 6,670 kilometers. The Amazon River in South America is the second longest, but because it is a younger river, it carries more water than any other river in the world.

Lakes

Lakes are inland bodies of water. They may be either salt water or fresh water. Lakes need a consistent supply of water, usually from river drainage. They may or may not have a method of drainage. The Dead Sea has no drainage. All the lakes in the world make up only 0.05% of the world's total volume of water. In terms of geological time, lakes are considered transient and temporary. They can disappear if more water flows out than flows in. New ones can be formed.

Lakes form in nondraining depressions or basins whose outlets are above the lowest part of the depression. Many lakes are the result of glacier action. During ice ages, glaciers gouge and scour depressions in the bedrock. These depressions provide nondraining basins for the meltwater to collect. Glaciers also produce dams by depositing debris across the drainage paths of streams.

In areas of low precipitation and high evaporation, some substances can become concentrated in lakes. Water that flows into the lakes often carries dissolved minerals. If the mineral is sodium chloride, saltwater lakes form. Dissolved sulfates create bitter lakes, carbonates crate alkali lakes, and borates create borax lakes. In North America most salt lakes are found in the great Basin area of the western U.S. because there are no drainage outlets to the ocean. The only escape for water is through evaporation.

The world's largest network of freshwater lakes is the Great Lakes. Since they are freshwater, they are not seas as the terms sea and ocean refer to saltwater bodies of water. The largest freshwater lake by volume is Lake Baikal in southern Siberia. It is 7 kilometers deep (the Grand Canyon is 1 km deep) and contains 20% of the world's fresh water.

 *Groundwater*

Precipitation that soaks into the ground through small pores or openings becomes groundwater. Gravity causes groundwater to move through interconnected porous rock formations from higher to lower elevations. The upper surface of the zone saturated with groundwater is the water table. A swamp is an area where the water table is at the surface. Sometimes the land dips below the water table and these areas fill with water forming lakes, ponds or streams. Groundwater that flows out from underground onto the surface is called a spring.

Permeable rocks filled with water are called aquifers. When a layer of permeable rock is trapped between two layers of impermeable rock, an aquifer is formed. Groundwater fills the pore spaces in the permeable rock. Layers of limestone are common aquifers. Groundwater is collected in reservoirs.

Groundwater provides drinking water for 53% of the population in the United States. Much groundwater is clean enough to drink without any type of treatment. Impurities in the water are filtered out by the rocks and soil through which it flows. However, many groundwater sources are becoming contaminated. Septic tanks, broken pipes, agricultural fertilizers, garbage dumps, rainwater runoff, and leaking underground tanks pollute groundwater. Toxic chemicals from farmland mix with groundwater. Removal of large volumes of groundwater can cause the collapse of soil and rock underground, causing the ground to sink. Along shorelines, excessive depletion of underground water supplies allows the intrusion of salt water into the fresh water field. Then the groundwater supply becomes undrinkable.

Groundwater usually contains large amounts of dissolved minerals, especially if the water flows through limestone. As groundwater drips through the roof of a cave, gases dissolved in the water can escape into the air. A deposit of calcium carbonate is left behind. Stalactites are icicle-like structures of calcium carbonate that hang from the roofs of caves. Water that falls on a constant spot on the cave floor and evaporates leaving a deposit of calcium carbonate builds a stalagmite.

Large features formed by dissolved limestone (calcium carbonate), include sinkholes, caves, and caverns. Sinkholes are funnel-shaped depressions created by dissolved limestone. Many sinkholes started life as a limestone cavern. Erosion weakens the cavern roof causing it to collapse, forming a sinkhole.

🎓 Glaciers

A glacier is a large, slow-moving river of ice, formed from compacted layers of snow. Gravity is the force that moves a glacier. Glacial ice is the largest reservoir of fresh water on Earth, and second to oceans as the largest reservoir of total water.

Geologic features created by glaciers include end, lateral, ground and medial moraines that form from glacially transported rocks and debris; V-shaped valleys changed to U-shaped valleys, often with cirques at their heads; and the glacier fringe which is the area where the glacier has recently melted into water.

After an episode of glaciations, the glaciers melt and retreat and leave behind piles of unsorted rock debris known as till. A drumlin is an oval-shaped mound of till. Its tip points in the direction that the glacier was moving. The first thing that happens to regolith or till is the leaching out of a variety of ions as water interacts with the mineral surfaces in the rock.

A unique part of the hydrological system, glaciers cause a number of distinctive landscape features. One example is the striations that are left behind in areas where glaciers have been. Because large rocks and other sharp, heavy objects are trapped in the glacial ice, as a glacier moves through an area they will leave long streaks in the ground, all running in the same direction. These are referred to as striations.

Another landscape feature which results from glaciers is a U-shaped valley. When a river cuts through an area, the valley that results will end in a point, like a V. However, glaciers push through canyons and erode them into a U-shape.

A moraine is a glacially-formed accumulation of unconsolidated debris which could have been plucked off the valley floor as the glacier advanced or could have fallen as a result of frost wedging. The debris can be of any size -- as fine as flour all the way to large boulders. However, it is usually angular, showing little or no abrasion or wearing. Rocks can be carried great distances by glaciers. Studying moraines helps scientists to determine where a glacier started and what path it may have taken.

Lateral moraines are parallel ridges of till (unsorted rock of varying sizes) deposited along the sides of an alpine glacier. Lateral moraines are deposited on top of the glacier due to frost shattering of the valley walls. Lateral moraines stay tall because they protect the ice under them from melting. Medial moraines form when the lateral moraines of two glaciers merge together. They, thus, form a ridge down the center of the combined glaciers.

Ground moraines are till-covered areas with irregular topography and no ridges. They often appear as gently rolling hills or plains. The till of these areas accumulated under the ice (by lodging there) and was deposited as the glacier retreated. End moraines (or terminal moraines) are debris deposited at the snout or end of the glacier and show the shape of the glacier's terminus. Glaciers act like a conveyor belt carrying debris from the top of the glacier to the bottom where it deposits the debris as the ice melts. End moraine size and shape is determined by how long the glacier stays in one place and if it advances or retreats after that.

A temperate glacier is at the melting point throughout the year. The ice of polar glaciers is always below the freezing point so the only mass loss is through sublimation (direct ice to atmosphere evaporation). Sub-polar glaciers have a seasonal melting time near the surface with some internal drainage.

The dry snow zone is a region of the glacier where no melting occurs, even in the summer. The percolation zone is an area with some surface melting. It is called percolation because the meltwater percolates into the snowpack and is refrozen. The wet snow zone is the region where all of the snow deposited since the end of the previous summer has been raised to 0°C. And the superimposed ice zone is where meltwater refreezes forming a continuous mass of ice.

The accumulation zone is the upper part of a glacier which receives most of the snowfall. It accounts for 60-70% of the glacier's surface area. The depth of the ice of this part of the glacier exerts a downward force which causes deep erosion of rock. After the glacier is gone, this part of the glacier leaves large bowl-shaped depressions called cirques.

The other end of the glacier is its foot or terminus. This is the deposition or ablation zone, an area where there is more melting than accumulation, so all the sediment is deposited. Where the glacier thins to nothing is the ice front.

Melting ice forms a stream, called a meltwater stream, that flows from the end of the glacier. This stream carries away sand and gravel which are deposited in long, trainlike deposits called valley trains. The meltwater may also form small lakes and ponds near the glacier. Sediments deposited by rivers of glacial meltwater in a fan-shaped area ahead of the terminal moraine form very fertile areas called outwash plains.

Glacial striations are long, linear rock scratches that follow a glacier's direction of movement. Chatter marks are divots in the rock. Glacial erratics are rounded boulders that were left by a melting glacier. These may be seen perched precariously on exposed rock faces of a very different type of rock after glacial retreat.

 # *Alpine Glaciers*

Alpine glaciers are found in mountain terrains. The smallest alpine glaciers form in mountain valleys and are called valley glaciers. Larger glaciers, called ice caps, can cover an entire mountain, a mountain chain, or a volcano. Ice caps feed outlet glaciers which are extensions of ice into valleys below. Alpine glaciers move down a mountain by gravity.

 # *Continental Glaciers*

Continental glaciers cover large areas that are not necessarily mountains but can include mountains. Antarctica and Greenland are the only places where continental glaciers exist today. The volume of ice in these sheets is so large that if the Greenland ice sheet melted, it would raise the sea levels around the world by 6 meters (20 feet) and if the Antarctica sheet melted, it would raise sea levels 65 meters (210 feet).

Plateau glaciers cover some plateaus and high-altitude areas. They resemble continental glaciers but on a much smaller scale. Plateau glaciers are found on Iceland, large islands in the Arctic Ocean, and from southern British Columbia to western Alaska.

Tidewater glaciers are glaciers that flow into the sea. As the ice reaches the sea, pieces break off, or clave, forming icebergs. Since most tidewater glaciers calve above sea level, a huge splash occurs when the iceberg strikes the water. If the water is deep, glaciers can calve underwater, causing the iceberg to suddenly seem to explode up out of the water. One of the longest tidewater glaciers is the Hubbard Glacier of Alaska with a calving face over 10 kilometers long.

Ice Ages

An ice age is a period of long-term reduction in the temperature of Earth's climate which results in an expansion of the continental glaciers and alpine glaciers. At least three ice ages have left evidences over the earth. There are three types of evidence: geological evidence such as rock scouring and scratching, moraines, deposition of till and glacial erratic, and valley cutting; chemical evidence such as variations in the ratios of isotopes in sedimentary rock; and paleontological evidence such as changes in the distribution of fossils.

The earliest ice age appears to have occurred 2.7 to 2.3 billion years ago during the Paleogne Period. It is known as the Huronian Ice Age. The earliest, well-documented ice age occurred 850 to 630 million years ago (during the Proterozoic Period) and probably produced Snowball Earth, an ice cover over the entire globe. A minor ice age probably occurred from 460 to 430 million years ago with extensive polar ice caps.

About 40 million years ago, the ice sheet in Antarctica began, starting a new ice age. Over the last 3 million years, there have been cycles of glaciations with ice sheets advancing and retreating on 40,000-100,000-year time scales. The most recent of these ended about 10,000 years ago.

 Oceanic Systems

Earth's surface is 71% water, most of which is found in the earth-encircling ocean. Seawater and ice make up 99.35% of all the water on Earth. The volume of the oceans is more than one billion cubic kilometers.

The terms sea and ocean both refer to saltwater bodies. A sea is smaller than an ocean. A sea or ocean can contain other seas. The Mediterranean Sea contains seven smaller seas. When the term "the seven seas" is used, it refers to the known world of the fifteenth century mapmakers. The seven seas they put on their maps were the Mediterranean Sea, the Red Sea, the East African Sea, the West African Sea, the China Sea, the Persian Gulf, and the Indian Ocean. Geographers today refer to five oceans: Pacific, Atlantic, Indian, Southern, and Arctic. However, there are only three ocean basins: the large Pacific, the Atlantic, and the small Indian. The water from all the oceans and seas interconnects and flows around and over the world.

World weather patterns are greatly influenced by ocean surface currents in the upper layer of the ocean. Surface currents are river-like bodies of water that do not extend very deeply under the surface of the ocean. These currents continuously move along the ocean surface in specific directions, usually long distances in huge curved paths.

Ocean currents that flow deep below the surface are called sub-surface currents. These currents are influenced by such factors as the location of landmasses in the current's path and the earth's rotation. These currents flow in opposite directions from surface currents and travel much more slowly. Deep currents are generated by differences in densities of ocean waters rather than by the wind.

Differences in water density can create ocean currents. Water found near the bottom of oceans is the coldest and the densest. Water tends to flow from a denser area to a less dense area. Currents that flow because of a difference in the density of the ocean water are called density currents. Water with a higher salinity is denser than water with a lower salinity. Water that has salinity different from the surrounding water may form a density current.

Surface currents are caused by winds and are classified by temperature. Cold currents originate in Polar regions and flow through surrounding water that is measurably warmer. Those currents with a higher temperature than the surrounding water are called warm currents and can be found near the equator. These currents follow swirling routes around the ocean basins and the equator. Ocean currents carry vast amounts of heat energy from the equator toward the poles.

The Gulf Stream and the California Current are the two main surface currents that flow along the coastlines of the United States. The Gulf Stream is a warm current in the Atlantic Ocean that carries warm water from the equator to the northern parts of the Atlantic Ocean. The Gulf Stream carries warm water north along the coast of the U.S.. As it moves north, it cools and becomes denser. Then it sinks into the deep sea near Greenland. When it sinks, it pulls more water northward to fill its place, creating a pattern of movement similar to a conveyor belt. The Gulf Stream was studied and named by Benjamin Franklin. The California Current is a cold current that originates in the Arctic regions and flows southward along the west coast of the United States.

The movement of an ocean current in one direction or another is influenced by the Coriolis effect. The Coriolis effect is due to the rotation of the earth. Ocean currents generated by winds move in a clockwise direction in the Northern Hemisphere and in a counterclockwise direction in the Southern Hemisphere.

The North Atlantic acts as a giant heat pump that cyclically warms and cools the atmosphere over the course of decades. The eastern part of the Atlantic Ocean is salty due to the emptying of the Mediterranean Sea which is shallow. The western part is relatively fresh. As the Gulf Stream pushes warm water into the North Atlantic a high-pressure region is created. The clockwise flow out of the region draws fresh water in from the west. The lighter (less salty) water does not sink easily so it slows the Gulf Stream. The northward flow of heat energy is reduced, so the water cools and starts sinking again. That creates a low-pressure zone which draws water in a counterclockwise direction, getting saltier water which is denser and sinks faster. One slow-down-speed-up cycle takes 40-60 years.

The movement of ocean water is caused by the wind, the sun's heat energy (convection), the earth's rotation, the moon's gravitational pull on earth, and underwater earthquakes. Most ocean waves are caused by the impact of winds. Wind blowing over the surface of the ocean transfers energy (friction) to the water and causes waves to form.

Waves are also formed by seismic activity on the ocean floor. A wave formed by an undersea volcanic eruption or earthquake is called a seismic sea wave, or a tsunami. These powerful waves can be very destructive, with wave heights of 30 meters or more near the shore. The crest of a wave is its highest point. The trough of a wave is its lowest point. The distance from wave top to wave top is the wavelength. The wave period is the time between the crests of two successive waves.

Waves "break" as they approach the shore and interact with the seafloor. The strength of the wind and the slope of the beach determine the shape of a breaking wave. (See Coasts for those descriptions.) The water particles in the wave move in a circular pattern that becomes more compressed and elliptical as it nears the shore. The particles slow in the trough but not in the crest, until eventually the crest overtakes the rest of the wave and spills over.

Extremely large waves are caused by the winds of hurricanes and other storms. The Beaufort Scale, which ranges from 0 to 12, is commonly used to quantify the strength of the wind. For example, a wind of 0 is a calm day. A wind of 6 is a strong breeze which produces waves of 3 meters in height (9-10 feet). Hurricane force winds are measured at 12 and produce 14-meter (50-ft) waves.

🎓 *Structural Geology*

The Earth's crust is always moving and changing. Wherever the rocks of the crust can be seen, evidence of rock movement can be seen. Some movements like earthquakes are rapid and large. Some movements happen slowly and continuously.

Sedimentary rock beds are separated by surfaces called bedding planes which are usually horizontal when the rocks are first formed. Many of the ancient sedimentary rocks are arranged at various angles to the horizontal and often to each other. Some appear vertical or even upside down.

The force that produces rock movement is called stress. Rock reacts to stress by changing its shape or volume or both. These deformations are called strain. Rocks have three strain responses: elastic deformation, plastic deformation, and rupture. In elastic deformation, the substance returns to its original shape and volume when the stress is removed. The deformation is proportional to the stress. In plastic deformation the substance undergoes a continuous change of shape and does not recover its original volume or shape. Usually the deformation is elastic up to a critical point (yield point). A rock will rupture or break apart if the pressure or stress becomes too great or the rocks are too hard to respond in a plastic or elastic way.

When rocks are deformed out of their original shape, they assume new patterns referred to as structural features. These features are joints, folds, faults, and unconformities. To describe the position in space of the rocks making up such structural features, geologists use two special measurements: dip and strike. The dip is the acute angle that a tilted rock layer makes with an imaginary horizontal plane. The direction of strike is always at right angles to the direction of the dip. The strike is the orientation of a line formed by the intersection of the bed with the horizontal plane.

Magma often forces its way into layers of sedimentary rock. When it hardens, it forms an igneous intrusion. The igneous intrusion is younger than the rock through which it passes. Igneous rock that forms on the surface is called an igneous extrusion. Igneous extrusions are younger than the layers underneath them.

Joints

The most common structural feature of rocks exposed at the surface is a joint. This is simply a break in the rock material without any relative movement of the rock on either side. Joints may have any orientation but in any given rock mass, joints tend to occur in sets with the fractures somewhat parallel to each other.

Joints may be a result of compression, tension or shear stress. Compression is a squeezing together type of force in which rocks move both up and down due to the sideways (sometimes torsional) squeezing. (Think of squeezing a ball of clay in your hand and having some of it squirt out at the top and some squirt out at the bottom.) A pulling apart force produces tension. Tension joints form a regular pattern at right angles to the tension. Both compression and tension produce strain and change the volume of rocks. Shearing, on the other hand, changes the shape but not the volume of the rocks as one block of rock is pushed past another.

Faults

Faults are fractures in the earth's crust which have been created by either tension or compression forces transmitted through the crust. The rupture point is exceeded. These forces are produced by the movement of separate blocks of crust. Earthquakes occur along faults. Fault movement leads to mountain building and volcanoes.

Faults are categorized on the basis of the relative movement between the blocks on both sides of the fault plane. The movement can be horizontal, vertical or oblique.

If the fracture, or fault plane, dips at some angle from the vertical, the mass of rock above the fault plane is called the hanging wall and the one beneath it the foot wall. Faults may be described on the basis of the relative movement of the foot wall to the hanging wall.

A dip-slip fault occurs when the movement of the plates is vertical and opposite (one part goes up and the other goes down). The displacement is in the direction of the inclination, or dip, of the fault. Dip-slip faults are classified as normal faults when the rock above the fault plane moves down relative to the rock below.

A normal fault is one in which the hanging wall has moved downward in relation to the foot wall. Normal faults are the result of tension, or pulling apart.

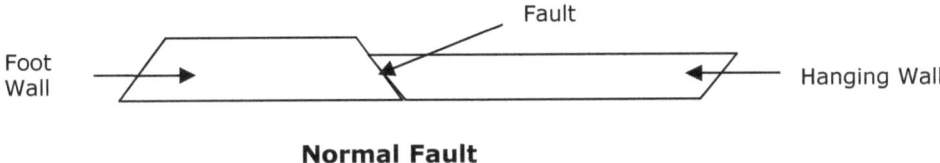

Normal Fault

Reverse faults are created when the hanging wall has moved upward relative to the foot rock below. Reverse faults are the result of compression. Reverse faults having a very low angle to the horizontal are also referred to as thrust faults.

Reverse Fault

Faults in which the dominant displacement is horizontal movement along the trend or strike (length) of the fault are called strike-slip faults. These can be left lateral or right lateral. If you were walking along a road and had to jog to the right to get to the rest of the road, you would be witnessing a right lateral strike-slip fault. When a large strike-slip fault is associated with plate boundaries it is called a transform fault. The San Andreas Fault in California is a well-known transform fault.

Faults that have both vertical and horizontal movement are called oblique-slip faults.

When a block moves vertically downward between two faults, the structure is called a graben. If this forms a topographical feature on the surface, it is a rift valley. Death Valley in California is a rift valley. The valley of the Dead Sea in Israel and Jordan is an example of an active rift valley. The faults appear to be continuing their movement since the Jordan River deposits tons of sand and mud in the Dead Sea each year, but the Dead Sea never gets any shallower.

If a block is left upstanding as the rock masses at each side are downfaulted, the result is a horst. A geomorphological feature produced like this is called a block mountain.

Unconformities

In many places younger rocks are separated from older rocks by surfaces of erosion or of nondeposition. Such surfaces are called unconformities. They represent events in Earth history but events which are not preserved as rock material. Geologists recognize angular unconformities, disconformities, and nonconformities. In an angular unconformity there are two series of rock layers that meet in a sharp angle. With a disconformity, the two series of rock layers are parallel but there is an obvious line of erosion between them. And a nonconformity is an unconformity that develops when massive igneous rocks are exposed to erosion and then covered by sedimentary rock layers.

All three types of unconformities are found in the Grand Canyon. There is a nonconformity between the non–sedimentary basement schists and everything above. An angular unconformity lies between the downfaulted block of Precambrian sedimentary rock and the Cambrian sequence above it. A disconformity lies between the horizontal Cambrian and Devonian strata.

Folds

Crustal movements may press horizontal layers of sedimentary rock together from the sides, squeezing them into wavelike folds. Up-folded sections of rock are called anticlines (they have an "A" shape); down-folded sections of rock are called synclines ("U" shape). In an eroded anticline the oldest beds are in the center and in an eroded syncline the youngest beds will be seen in the center of the fold. Anticlines form ridges and hills while synclines form the valleys. The Appalachian Mountains (from Canada to Alabama) are an example of folded mountains with long ridges and valleys in a series of anticlines and synclines formed by folded rock layers.

Even though an anticline is an upward fold, it is not always higher than the surrounding land. The compression may not be great enough to bring the fold to the surface. Or the folds may be covered by new rock layers. Or the ridge may have eroded.

 *Interior of the Earth*

The core, the center, of the earth is divided into the outer core and inner core. The density of the core is 10-12 grams per cubic centimeter which is considerable denser than iron at the surface of the earth at 2.5 grams per cubic centimeter. This is due to the increased pressure at the core. The inner core is thought to be a solid iron or solid iron-nickel. The earth's magnetic field is explained by understanding the iron core. The outer core is believed to be molten iron or a molten iron-nickel with some lighter elements like silicon, sulfur and oxygen.

The layer between the core and the crust is called the mantle. It is about 2900 km deep and is basically solid with some localized partial melting of the ferromagnesian silicates in the outermost layer. Below that are oxides and silicates of iron, magnesium, silicon and some minor elements which are all solids.

The lower mantle is the area from 2900 km to somewhere between 200 and 400 km below the earth's crust. Here there is a transition zone where earthquake wave velocities change. The change appears to be due to phase changes – changes in crystalline structure without changes in composition.

The boundary between the mantle and the crust is called the Mohorovicic discontinuity, or Moho. Just under this is the upper mantle which is made up of the lithosphere and asthenosphere. The lithosphere is a rigid layer that extends to a depth of about 100 kilometers. It contains the dozen or so massive plates upon which the continental and ocean basin crust ride as well as the crust itself. The asthenosphere is considered a low velocity zone because earthquake waves decrease in velocity as they move through it. This area is less rigid than the lithosphere. The upper mantle continues below the asthenosphere where it is very soft and partially molten.

Under the continents and oceans is the earth's crust which varies from 10 to 50 (sometimes considered 5-60 km) kilometers. Under oceans it is quite thin, but under continental mountains it becomes its thickest. However, the average density below oceans is 3 grams per cubic centimeter while it is only 2.2 grams per cubic centimeter under continents. The crust's density increases with increasing depth. This density difference occurs because of a difference in composition.

The earth's crust is composed almost entirely of different combinations of the eight most common elements: oxygen (46.6%), silicon (27.7%), aluminum (8.13%), iron (5.00%), calcium (3.63%), sodium (2.82%), potassium (2.59%), and magnesium (2.09%). Oceanic crust consists mainly of basaltic rocks rich in the heavier common metals like iron and magnesium. It is similar to the upper mantle. Continental crust is composed of a variety of rock types, but the predominant rocks are granites which are rich in silicates (silicon and oxygen).

All crust is recycled as a result of geological processes, but the average age of rock in continental crust is about 650 million years while oceanic crust is only about 60 million years. This difference is best explained by the theory of plate tectonics. Accordingly, oceanic crust appears to be recycled by subduction more frequently than continental crust.

Plate Tectonics

Data obtained from many sources led scientists to develop the theory of plate tectonics. This theory is the most current model that explains not only the movement of the continents, but also the changes in the earth's crust caused by internal forces. The basic concept for plate tectonics began with Alfred Wegener in the early 1900s. His theory of continental drift held that all continents were once one great continent which he called Pangaea. He felt that at some time, the continents began to break apart and float apart.

Evidences of plate tectonics include fossils, mountains, and glaciers. Fossils are preserved remains or evidence of plant or animal life. In most cases these evidences – bones, impressions, shells, leaves – were left in mud or sand and became a part of sedimentary rock. Fossils of the same animals and plants from the same time period have been found in rocks in countries that today are very far from each other – Australia, India, and South Africa.

The Cape Mountains of South Africa and the mountains near Buenos Aires, Argentina, are very similar folded mountains which in both cases end in the ocean. Not only is it very unusual for mountains to end in an ocean, but for two ranges that are so similar to end in the ocean makes them appear to have been connected at one time.

Glacier deposits found in South America, Africa, India, Australia, and Antarctica seem to match. The direction of flow of the glacier appears to have been the same on Africa and South America.

As scientists started studying the oceans in the late 1950s, the similarities to and differences from continents and other oceans became apparent. All oceans have mid-ocean ridges which form long chains of huge mountains. Rocks next to mid-ocean ridges are younger than those farther away, with the youngest rocks in the center of the ridges. Therefore, the idea of ocean floor spreading was born.

In today's theory the entire earth's lithosphere is broken into nine large sections, or plates, and several small ones. Plates are rigid blocks of earth's crust and upper mantle. The major plates are named after the continents they are "transporting."

The plates float on and move with a layer of hot, plastic-like rock in the upper mantle. Geologists believe that the heat currents circulating within the mantle cause this plastic zone of rock to slowly flow, carrying along the overlying crustal plates. In this way, the surface of the earth is in constant motion.

The major lithospheric plates are named for surface features found on them. The largest plate is the Pacific Plate which includes about one-fifth of the earth's surface. The other plates are the North American, South American, Eurasian, African, Australian, and Antarctic Plates. The North American includes North America but extends into the Atlantic Ocean as does the Eurasian. There are also several smaller plates. For example, the Arabian plate includes the Arabian peninsula, the Red Sea, and the Persian Gulf. The Pacific plate is the only one that does not contain any continental crust.

One of the many unique features of the Earth which make it difficult for astronomer's to determine whether or not any other planet is capable of sustaining life to the extent that the earth is the presence of tectonic plates. The tectonic plates are important for a number of reasons, such as the fact that they allow the earth to maintain a stable internal temperature and are responsible for the magnetic poles (which help protect against solar flares). Although it is not sure whether tectonic plates are truly essential in the development of life, they do give the Earth many unique properties. So far, no other planets have been discovered to have active tectonic plates (although there is some evidence that Mars may have once had them in its early history).

Plate Movements

The movement of the plates may be related to convection currents within the earth. A convection current is the movement of gases or liquids caused by differences in temperatures. Major plate separation lines lie along the ocean floors. Molten rock rises, separating (diverging) the plates, continuously forming new ocean crust and creating new and taller mountain ridges under the ocean. The Mid-Atlantic is one of the major areas of divergence. Currents of hot mantle rock rise and separate at this point of divergence, creating new oceanic crust at the rate of 2 to 10 centimeters per year. The Mid-Atlantic Range which runs north to south through the Atlantic Ocean basin divides it into two nearly equal parts and shows evidence from mapping of such deep-ocean floor changes.

Movement of these crustal plates creates areas where the plates converge as well as areas where the plates diverge. Convergence is when the oceanic crust collides with either another oceanic plate or a continental plate. The oceanic crust sinks forming an enormous trench known as a subduction zone and generating volcanic activity. Portions of the lithosphere are dragged into the mantle. Then some of this material melts and volcanoes erupt. In time, a series of volcanic islands such as the Aleutian Islands is formed parallel to the trench.

Convergence also includes continent to continent plate collisions. When two plates slide past one another a transform fault is created. These movements produce many major features of the earth's surface, such as mountain ranges, volcanoes, and earthquake zones. Most of these features are located at plate boundaries, where the plates interact by spreading apart, pressing together, or sliding past each other. These movements are very slow, averaging only a few centimeters a year. The crustal movement which is identified by plates sliding sideways past each other produces a plate boundary characterized by major faults that are capable of unleashing powerful earthquakes. The San Andreas Fault forms such a boundary between the Pacific Plate and the North American Plate.

When two plates are sliding past each other, rather than pushing into each other or pulling apart from each other, the result is a transform plate boundary, or a transform fault. Transform faults are most commonly found in the ocean, but one very prominent example is the San Andreas Fault in California. The only real result of a transform fault is a large number of earthquakes and the plates move. Transform faults are nearly always connected at the ends with other types of plate boundaries. For example, a transform fault may occur as a mid-oceanic ridge pushes the crust material it produces past other sections of the ocean floor which are not part of the ridge.

When two tectonic plates collide, a possible result is subduction. Subduction refers to situations in which one of the plates is pushed beneath the other. This occurs in the case of ocean-ocean and ocean-continent collisions. When subduction occurs it results in a number of occurrences. For example, as the plate is pushed down into the mantle it will result in increased volcanic activity about the subducted plate. Therefore, volcanic activity along a plate boundary is a sign of subduction. Another result of subduction is numerous earthquakes, and the emergence of mountain ranges (as one plate is subducted it will also push up on the plate above it, causing mountains). Trenches are another common feature of subduction zones.

Plate Boundaries

Boundaries form between spreading plates where the crust is forced apart in a process called rifting. Rifting occurs at mid-ocean ridges when lava erupts from a valley or rift that runs the length of the ridge. Rifting can also take place within a continent, splitting the continent into smaller landmasses that drift away from each other, thereby forming an ocean basin between them. The Red Sea is a product of rifting. As the ocean floor spreading takes place, lava cools and hardens to form rock which is added to the edges of the separating plates. In this way the plates are pushed apart and grow larger, and the ocean basin widens. This is the process that broke up the super continent Pangaea and created the Atlantic Ocean.

Even though the ocean floors are spreading, the earth is not getting any larger. Older rocks of the ocean floor get pushed deep into the earth along trenches which are long V-shaped valleys. This often happens at boundaries between plates, near the edges of oceans. When a plate of ocean crust collides with a plate of continental crust, the more dense oceanic plate slides under the lighter continental plate and plunges into the mantle. This process is called subduction, and the site where it takes place is called a subduction zone. There is a balance (a type of equilibrium) between the building of new plate material at the ocean ridges and the destroying of old plate material at the trenches.

At plate boundaries where two oceanic crusts are diverging a phenomenon occurs which is known as sea floor spreading. As the plates pull apart, volcanic activity occurs and basalt pushes up through the diverging plates to form new ocean crust. This means that the youngest rocks will be located near the actual plate boundary and older rocks will radiate out parallel to it in either direction (the oldest rocks, therefore, would be nearest to continents). The most well-known divergent ocean boundary is the Mid-Atlantic Ridge in the middle of the Atlantic Ocean. Determining the rate of sea floor spreading requires knowledge of the distance between two points, and the difference in their ages.

For example, a point on the ocean floor is 2 kilometers from the plate boundary is dated to be 10,000 years old. In this example, the two points would be the plate boundary, corresponding to distance zero and age zero for the sake of simplicity, and the known point. Because the movement happens so slowly the measurements are usually converted to centimeters, and then the rate of seafloor spreading would be found by dividing distance by time. The resulting calculation would be 200,000cm/10,000yrs=20 cm/yr.

It is at plate boundaries that the majority of volcanoes and earthquakes take place. Faults and earthquakes go hand-in-hand just as volcanoes and mountain-building are related.

While the result of divergent ocean-ocean boundaries is sea floor spreading, when two ocean plates collide the result is much different. At a convergent ocean-ocean boundary, whichever of the ocean plates is older (and correspondingly more dense) will subduct, and be pushed underneath the other. This will result in volcanic activity above the subducted plate, and the result will be the formation of an island arc. It is important to distinguish island arcs from island chains. Island chains are straight and form over hot spots in the mantle. Although island arcs consist of a chain of islands, the chain is curved and they form at convergent ocean-ocean boundaries. Examples of island arcs include Japan and the Aleutian Islands.

Environmental Geography

As water moves through wetlands (marshes and swamps) matter suspended in the water is trapped by plant roots or settles out as sediment. Marshes and swamps provide a service to humans and animals by filtering and cleaning polluted water. They also provide a home to a great variety of wildlife. The past century has seen the loss of huge amounts of wetlands worldwide to "provide" for projects such as farming, housing, grazing, industry, and even parkland.

The most important agent of geological erosion is homo sapiens – us. Building dams, bridges, roads, and other parts of civilization seems to require the blasting of mountainsides. Rock and ore quarries are huge holes in the ground. Strip mines for coal and ore remove huge amounts of rock and soil. Forests are cleared and rocks are moved to provide for farming and grazing. By removing these upper layers of humus, roots, and grasses, the next layers are more easily washed or blown away and leave areas barren and untillable.

Even attempts to irrigate dry land can sometimes cause more problems than are solved. For example, when rivers flowing into the Aral Sea were diverted for irrigation, the Aral Sea began to dry up and the exposed salt was blown over the land which made it unfit for cultivation.

Coastal land can be easily affected by the attempts of man. If breakwaters are built (to protect harbors), they cause sandbars to form in unexpected places and even contribute to the harbor not being deep enough to be a harbor after a while. If sand and gravel are removed from a beach area, the pattern of coastal currents is changed. This can affect nearby villages in many ways – by causing the currents to wash the land out from beneath the village, by taking fish to a different area (removal of food or their form of making a living), or by washing other things into the village.

"Acid rain" is a broad term referring to a mixture of wet and dry deposition (deposited material) from the atmosphere containing higher than normal amounts of nitric and sulfuric acids. The precursors, or chemical forerunners, of acid rain formation result from both natural sources, such as volcanoes and decaying vegetation, and man-made sources, primarily emissions of sulfur dioxide (SO_2) and nitrogen oxides (NO_x) resulting from fossil fuel combustion. In the United States, roughly 2/3 of all SO_2 and 1/4 of all NO_x come from electric power generation that relies on burning fossil fuels, like coal. Acid rain occurs when these gases react in the atmosphere with water, oxygen, and other chemicals to form various acidic compounds. The result is a mild solution of sulfuric acid and nitric acid. When sulfur dioxide and nitrogen oxides are released from power plants and other sources, prevailing winds blow these compounds across state and national borders, sometimes over hundreds of miles.

As this acidic water flows over and through the ground, it affects a variety of plants and animals. In areas where the weather is dry, the acid chemicals may become incorporated into dust or smoke and fall to the ground through dry deposition, sticking to the ground, buildings, homes, cars, and trees. Dry deposited gases and particles can be washed from these surfaces by rainstorms, leading to increased runoff. This runoff water makes the resulting mixture more acidic. About half of the acidity in the atmosphere falls back to earth through dry deposition.

Acid rain causes acidification of lakes and streams and contributes to the damage of trees at high elevations (for example, red spruce trees above 2,000 feet) and many sensitive forest soils. In addition, acid rain accelerates the decay of building materials and paints as well as irreplaceable buildings, statues, and sculptures that are part of a nation's cultural heritage. Prior to falling to the earth, sulfur dioxide (SO_2) and nitrogen oxide (NO_x) gases and their particulate matter derivatives—sulfates and nitrates—contribute to visibility degradation and harm public health.

Carbon dioxide, water vapor, and other gases pumped into the atmosphere as a side effect of industry change the balance of atmospheric gases and produce the greenhouse effect. The greenhouse effect takes place when the heat from the sun can pass through to the Earth's surface but the re-radiated heat finds it difficult to escape. As a result, the climate begins to warm more and more each year.

Studies have shown that freon, a propellant in aerosol sprays prior to 1978, was destroying the ozone layer and allowing too much ultraviolet light to reach the earth. When this happens, people get skin cancer more easily, crops are damaged, and changes take place in the weather and climate. Newer propellants such as nitrogen oxides and bromofluorocarbons may also damage the ozone layer or speed the greenhouse effect.

Every day tons of industrial wastes are produced. Many of these wastes are highly toxic. They can cause cancer, skin rashes, respiratory problems, and death. Some emit toxic fumes, others are toxic to the touch, and still others combine with elements in the soil or water to create toxic substances which can harm water that is used for drinking water or soil used for growing food for people or animals. Disposal methods for these wastes has become a huge problem. Nearly every method has drawbacks and opponents as well as advantages and proponents.

 Landscapes and Weathering

The landscapes that exist on earth today are a combined result of the effects of weather, erosion, tectonic motion, and human activity over time. Landscapes are often characterized by elevation. For example, the most common landscapes (or landforms) are mountains, plateaus, plains, and valleys. Mountains are massive rock formations with high elevations. Plateaus are level areas with fairly high elevations. Plains are low elevations areas characterized by long stretches of flat land. Valleys are the depressions in the earth's surface that exist between mountains.

The processes of weathering and erosion are also extremely important in shaping landscapes. Weathering describes the processes that wear away at rocks and change their characteristics. Weathering includes the forces of water, air, and chemicals as they alter the composition and characteristics of rocks and rock formations. Water contributes to the weathering process because as water flows over rocks, it chips and wears away at the sediments that compose them, and breaks them down. Air also contributes to the process because wind can wear away at the surface of the rock, and dries out the surface and environment. Finally, chemicals can both alter the composition of the rock, and break down bonds between different minerals.

The process of erosion is the process by which sediments are moved after weathering has occurred. The primary agent of erosion is water or the hydrologic cycle. Once chemicals, air, and water have broken rocks down and exposed the sediments, they can then be picked up by flowing water and transported away. Over time this process of weathering (breaking down the rock) and erosion (moving away the broken down sediments) is what causes different landforms to develop.

 Types of Caves

A cave is defined as a large, hollow, underground space. Generally caves are formed naturally, and can range in size from a space just large enough for a person to enter, to massive open caverns or series of rooms that run for miles. The size, composition, and location of caves is based on the cave type. There are four main types of caves: limestone caves, lava caves, sea caves, and ice caves.

By far the most common types of caves are limestone caves. These can be found across the United States and throughout the world. Although limestone caves are some of the largest and longest caves in the world, they form slowly over thousands of years. Limestone caves form as water mixes with chemicals to form what is essentially acid rain, which then wears at the cave walls over time and hollows out the cave.

The next most common type of caves are lava caves. These caves are found in highly volcanic regions. Lava caves form during eruptions when the outer layer of a lava flow hardens, but the inside remains molten. The molten part eventually flows out, leaving the hardened outer layer hollow and resulting in a lava cave. Although they do not have all of the same interesting geologic features of limestone caves (i.e., stalactites, stalagmites, and other formations) they can have interesting formations that formed as the lava dried.

Sea caves are relatively small caves that form facing an open ocean area. These caves tend to be small, and are created by the continual impact of ocean waves against a rock surface.

The final type of cave is an ice cave. Ice caves are created within glaciers when water flows under the frozen surface of the glacier and results in a hollow space within it. Both sea caves and ice caves are fairly rare in comparison to lava and limestone caves.

# Kettle and Kame

One type of topography which emerges as a result of retreating glacier is referred to as kettle and kame topography. Kettles and kames are two different and distinct land formations which are created in such areas. A kame forms where there is a hole in the ice. As streams flow off of the retreating glacier, sediments are deposited in the hole. As a result, hills are constructed from the sediments.

These are the kames. Kettles, on the other hand, form in an opposite manner when chunks of the glacier get left behind. These chunks can be covered with sediments and typically form into ponds or lakes once they eventually melt. Therefore, kettle and kame topography is characterized by the presences of hills and ponds or depressions.

 # Outwash Plain

A third type of land formation typical of retreating glaciers (in addition to kettles and kames) is the outwash plain. As you might expected form its name, an outwash plain is created by water flowing off of the glacier as it melts. The runoff, or outwash, will deposit sediments at the base of the glacier, resulting in a fan shaped mound (referred to as an alluvial fan) which gives way to a flat plain, or outwash plain.

 # Horst and Graben

Horst and graben are topographical features which develop when multiple faults run parallel to one another, resulting in elevated and depressed blocks of land. The presence of fault lines can cause an area to be elevated in two different ways. First, the land can be pushed up, so that the elevated land rises above its neighboring region which remains at the same elevation.

In cases such as this, the elevated area is referred to as a horst. Alternately, some areas of land may slide lower as the then elevated land around them remains at the same actual elevation. In this case, the depressions would be referred to as grabens. These grabens are also commonly referred to as rift valleys. Horsts and grabens may range in size from a few meters to many miles across.

 # Karst

A karst is essentially an underground aquifer. They are formed when a water supply (such as a pond or stream) encounters a region built on soluble rocks. The water wears away at the rocks forming numerous underground caverns and fissures. The land above these areas is often pitted with depressions and sinkholes as a result of fluctuations in the pressure and water supply of the fissures beneath. Karst regions are characterized by these common underground caverns, fissures, and streams, with the land above characterized by contamination of groundwater, unpredictable water supply, and sinkholes.

 Severe Weather

Various forms of severe weather phenomenon exist that are each caused by unique meteorological situations. These weather phenomena include thunder storms, tornadoes, hurricanes, earthquakes, volcanoes, heat waves and monsoons.

Thunder storms are storms which in addition to rain or another form of precipitation (if any precipitation occurs) generate lightning and thunder. Thunderstorms are caused when warm and humid air rises in areas that are already beginning to storm. Because of this condition, thunderstorms typically happen at the beginning of the evening because the surface of the land is still hot from the sun. Then, once the sun sets, the air begins to rise as the air above it becomes cooler due to the lack of the sun's heat.

Due to the fact that thunderstorms are caused by rising warm air, they are most common in Florida, and in inland areas. The Pacific coast of the United States and the remainder of the Atlantic coast have thunder storms fairly rarely because the temperatures in these areas are moderated by the presence of the ocean. However, in Florida because there is ocean both on the east and west there are actually more thunder storms. The cool ocean breezes move in from both sides, which forces the hot air up, rather than cooling the area.

Tornadoes

Tornadoes are violent wind storms where the wind circles into a rotating vortex formed from a cumulonimbus cloud. Tornadoes often begin as simple thunderstorms, but as high winds develop they transform into a tornado. Tornadoes primarily occur in the large, flat plains of the central United States. In terms of meteorological conditions, they are generated when cold air and warm air run into each other.

Tornadoes are most commonly found in the central United States, east of the Rocky Mountains. Cold air fronts head eastward off of the mountain range and meet with tropical warm fronts moving from the southeast. The region receiving the most tornadoes is called Tornado Alley and includes the states of Oklahoma, Nebraska, Kansas, and North and South Dakota.

Hurricanes

Hurricanes can be compared to a tornado which develops over water. Because water is so dangerous when it gets moving quickly (it is 1000 times denser and therefore 1000 times more destructive than air), hurricanes are among the most dangerous storms there are. Hurricanes are also known as typhoons and cyclones, and can occur in any tropical ocean. The violence of the hurricane is created when water becomes hot enough that it begins to condense in large quantities into water vapor (this happens at temperatures upwards of 80 degrees Fahrenheit).

For this reason they are common in late summer. Although hurricanes happen over water, they are extremely destructive to human populations because they create storm surges. Storm surges are storms and rising sea shores as a result of the hurricanes.

The most common location for hurricanes to occur is in the northwest part of the Pacific Ocean. However, they can also form in the western Caribbean, and in the United States will often form in the Gulf of Mexico. States bordering the Gulf of Mexico, therefore, are the most susceptible to hurricanes. For example, Florida, Texas, and all of the states in between.

Earthquakes

Earthquakes and volcanoes are the next major phenomenon. Earthquakes are caused by the movement of tectonic plates. Tectonics plates are plates which float atop a semi liquid layer of magma and shift across the surface of the earth. Although it is not visible to the naked eye, tectonic plates are in continual motion. This motion can be measured and witnessed through different geologic phenomenon such as earthquakes, the formation of mountains, and the eruption of volcanoes.

Earthquakes occur because as plates shift past each other, tension in the Earth's surface builds up. Plates can either pull apart, slide past each other, or push together. In each case, earthquakes result. Areas where plates border each other are called fault lines, and these are the areas where earthquakes happen. The most prominent fault lines in the United States include the San Andreas fault line in California. In fact, the majority of all earthquakes in the United States occur in California.

Volcanoes

The eruption of volcanoes is a spectacular and highly visible result of the movement of tectonic plates. The most noticeable area in which volcanoes occur as a result of tectonic motion is referred to as the ring of fire in the Pacific Ocean. The ring of fire is a giant loop of volcanoes that outline the Pacific Ocean, or more relevantly the pacific plate. These volcanoes run along the eastern coast of Asia, encompassing China, Japan, Indonesia, the Philippines, and New Zealand, and continues to the western coast of North and South America. Therefore, not only is California the most affected by earthquakes, but along with Hawaii, Oregon and Washington is the most susceptible to volcanic activity.

Heat Waves

Heat waves are long periods of intense heat. Although they are not a specific whether phenomenon, heat waves typically cause more fatalities than other types of weather phenomenon combined. Heat waves increase the risk of fires, and can wipe out crops and vegetation. When high humidity is also present it becomes unhealthy for people to be outdoors, and their health is put at risk.

Monsoons

Monsoons are periods of intense rainfall and flooding that are responsible for the majority of the rainfall in the tropical areas of Southeast Asia. Massive amounts of sustained rainfall result in the flooding of rivers and other bodies of water that can wipe out cities and communities. These monsoons are caused as a change in season results in a change in wind patterns. These produce longer, wetter seasons of rain.

Disease and Climate

A number of diseases are closely associated with warmer climates, which is one reason that global warming can be a worry in already tropical climates. Diseases that are associated with warm, moist climates are often referred to as tropical diseases. These diseases are often transmitted by parasites or insects, and commonly outbreak just after cooler periods in which these organisms briefly hibernate. Some diseases associated with tropical climates are yellow fever, malaria, dengue fever, and cholera.

Two terms that are commonly used in reference to disease are endemic and epidemic. It is important to understand the distinction between these two terms. The term endemic is used to describe a condition that is found in a specific geographic region and is recurring. In contrast, an epidemic describes a disease that spreads over a large space is a relatively rapid manner.

As a result, rather than being a continuous problem, it affects an unusually large number of people across geographic areas at the same time. Also as a result, epidemics tend to subside at some point, whereas endemics do not. For example, malaria is a disease that is commonly found in Africa as a result of a combination of climate and hygiene factors. It would be correct to say, therefore, that malaria is endemic to Africa. In contrast, an epidemic of the bubonic (black) plague in the 15th century wiped out nearly a third of the population of Europe.

Weather Patterns

One of the largest classifications relating to the difference in climates of different areas is whether it is a continental or maritime area. Continental weather patterns create a situation with positive feedback – in other words, the weather compounds on itself because of the topography. When the sun shines down on continental areas, the land soaks up and absorbs the heat, but it has no place to go. As a result the whole area becomes slightly warmer. When the sun goes down at night, the temperature will fall without the presence of sunlight.

On the other hand, maritime locations (i.e., locations near the sea) tend to have much more consistent temperatures. This is because during the day, the water will absorb and diffuse the heat throughout the day. This heat is pulled around by ocean currents and breezes. Then, when the sun goes down at night, winds will blow inland, pulling the warmer water temperatures towards the land. This creates more moderate and mild temperatures overall.

Ozone

Ozone is a gas that occurs both in the Earth's upper atmosphere and at ground level. Ozone can be "good" or "bad" for your health and the environment, depending on its location in the atmosphere.

HOW CAN OZONE BE BOTH GOOD AND BAD?

Ozone occurs in two layers of the atmosphere. The layer closest to the Earth's surface is the troposphere. Here, ground-level or "bad" ozone is an air pollutant that is harmful to breathe and it damages crops, trees and other vegetation. It is a main ingredient of urban smog. The troposphere generally extends to a level about six miles up, where it meets the second layer, the stratosphere. The stratosphere or "good" ozone layer extends upward from about 6 to 30 miles and protects life on Earth from the sun's harmful ultraviolet (UV) rays. Ozone (O3) is a form of oxygen which is important because it has the ability to absorb high energy radiation emitted by the sun, which can be harmful to people. The ozone layer of the atmosphere resides in the stratosphere. Because of this, temperature actually increases farther into the stratosphere.

The troposphere is the first layer of the atmosphere, and extends 10 miles up from the earth. This is the layer where weather occurs, meaning that there is a lot of vertical movement as water falls as precipitation, and later evaporates. This is quite different from the stratosphere which has virtually no vertical motion, so things remain there for long periods of time. Because there is no vertical motion within the stratosphere it is good that ozone is there. It can absorb the harmful radiation from the sun, without coming into contact with people. When there is ozone in the troposphere it can become dangerous. Since there is so much vertical motion it spreads throughout the layer, carrying the harmful radiation with it.

WHAT IS HAPPENING TO THE "GOOD" OZONE LAYER?

Ozone is produced naturally in the stratosphere. But this "good" ozone is gradually being destroyed by man-made chemicals referred to as ozone-depleting substances (ODS), including chlorofluorocarbons (CFCs), hydrochlorofluorocarbons (HCFCs), halons, methyl bromide, carbon tetrachloride, and methyl chloroform. These substances were formerly used and sometimes still are used in coolants, foaming agents, fire extinguishers, solvents, pesticides, and aerosol propellants. Once released into the air these ozone-depleting substances degrade very slowly. In fact, they can remain intact for years as they move through the troposphere until they reach the stratosphere. There they are broken down by the intensity of the sun's UV rays and release chlorine and bromine molecules, which destroy the "good" ozone. Scientists estimate that one chlorine atom can destroy 100,000 "good" ozone molecules.

Even though we have reduced or eliminated the use of many ODSs, their use in the past can still affect the protective ozone layer. Research indicates that depletion of the "good" ozone layer is being reduced worldwide. The thinning of the protective ozone layer can be observed using satellite measurements, particularly over the Polar Regions.

HOW DOES THE DEPLETION OF "GOOD" OZONE AFFECT HUMAN HEALTH AND THE ENVIRONMENT?

Ozone depletion can cause increased amounts of UV radiation to reach the Earth which can lead to more cases of skin cancer, cataracts, and impaired immune systems. Overexposure to UV is believed to be contributing to the increase in melanoma, the most fatal of all skin cancers. Since 1990, the risk of developing melanoma has more than doubled.

UV can also damage sensitive crops, such as soybeans, and reduce crop yields. Some scientists suggest that marine phytoplankton, which are the base of the ocean food chain, are already under stress from UV radiation. This stress could have adverse consequences for human food supplies from the oceans.

WHAT IS BEING DONE ABOUT THE DEPLETION OF "GOOD" OZONE?

The United States, along with over 180 other countries, recognized the threats posed by ozone depletion and in 1987 adopted a treaty called the Montreal Protocol to phase out the production and use of ozone-depleting substances.

The EPA has established regulations to phase out ozone-depleting chemicals in the United States. Warning labels must be placed on all products containing CFCs or similar substances and nonessential uses of ozone-depleting products are prohibited. Releases into the air of refrigerants used in car and home air conditioning units and appliances are also prohibited. Some substitutes to ozone-depleting products have been produced and others are being developed. If the United States and other countries stop producing ozone-depleting substances, natural ozone production should return the ozone layer to normal levels by about 2050.

WHAT CAUSES "BAD" OZONE?

Ground-level or "bad" ozone is not emitted directly into the air, but is created by chemical reactions between oxides of nitrogen (NOx) and volatile organic compounds (VOC) in the presence of sunlight. Emissions from industrial facilities and electric utilities, motor vehicle exhaust, gasoline vapors, and chemical solvents are some of the major sources of NOx and VOC.

At ground level, ozone is a harmful pollutant. Ozone pollution is a concern during the summer months because strong sunlight and hot weather result in harmful ozone concentrations in the air we breathe. Many urban and suburban areas throughout the United States have high levels of "bad" ozone. But many rural areas of the country are also subject to high ozone levels as winds carry emissions hundreds of miles away from their original sources.

HOW DOES "BAD" OZONE AFFECT HUMAN HEALTH AND THE ENVIRONMENT?

Breathing ozone can trigger a variety of health problems including chest pain, coughing, throat irritation, and congestion. It can worsen bronchitis, emphysema, and asthma. "Bad" ozone also can reduce lung function and inflame the lining of the lungs. Repeated exposure may permanently scar lung tissue.

Healthy people also experience difficulty breathing when exposed to ozone pollution. Because ozone forms in hot weather, anyone who spends time outdoors in the summer may be affected, particularly children, outdoor workers and people exercising. Millions of Americans live in areas where the national ozone health standards are exceeded.

Ground-level or "bad" ozone also damages vegetation and ecosystems. It leads to reduced agricultural crop and commercial forest yields, reduced growth and survivability of tree seedlings, and increased susceptibility to diseases, pests and other stresses such as harsh weather. In the United States alone, ground-level ozone is responsible for an estimated $500 million in reduced crop production each year. Ground-level ozone also damages the foliage of trees and other plants, affecting the landscape of cities, national parks and forests, and recreation areas.

WHAT IS BEING DONE ABOUT "BAD" OZONE?

Under the Clean Air Act, the EPA has set protective health-based standards for ozone in the air we breathe. The EPA, state, and cities have instituted a variety of multi-faceted programs to meet these health-based standards. Throughout the country, additional programs are being put into place to cut NOx and VOC emissions from vehicles, industrial facilities, and electric utilities. Programs are also aimed at reducing pollution by reformulating fuels and consumer/commercial products, such as paints and chemical solvents that contain VOC. Voluntary programs also encourage communities to adopt practices, such as carpooling, to reduce harmful emissions.

Universal Religion

An important classification when discussing different religions around the world is as either universalizing or non-universalizing. These definitions tend to be fairly straightforward. A religion is a universalizing (or universal) religion if it has the goal of spreading throughout the world. Religions which are aimed at preaching their message and converting as many people as possible are universal religions. For example, Christian religions are almost always universalizing. In fact, the religions that people encounter the most are universal religions. This is because the purpose of universal religions is to spread. Therefore they are more advertised and have a larger follower base than non-universal religions do. Islam and Buddhism are also examples of universal religions.

However, while universal religions are more common, there is one typical criticism of them – that they are too adaptable. This is because many people feel that by their nature they have a tendency to be more malleable and conforming. The criticism is, essentially, that universalizing religions adapt to be most attractive to the greatest number of individuals. As a result, they are changing and less meaningful.

In contrast to universal religions, non-universal religions are more self-contained. One of the most common examples of a non-universal religion is Judaism. Because the belief in Judaism is that only those who are the original Children of Israel will be saved, they do not have a great interest in converting other people to accept their beliefs.

 # Origins of Buddhism

The origins of Buddhism can be traced back to the 5th century BC in India. It is based on the teachings of a man named Siddhartha Gautama, who came to be known as Buddha – which literally means "enlightened." Buddha was raised in luxury as a prince. However, upon leaving his father's home on successive trips he witnessed various forms of human suffering (old age, death, illness, etc.). As a result, he came to the conclusion that luxury can only mask suffering and that pleasure is only temporary. The resulting theology of Buddhism that emerged was the goal of attaining a state of completely detachment or Nirvana, which constitutes a release from both suffering and pleasure.

 # Religion in India

The largest religion in India is by a wide margin Hinduism. According to data collected by the CIA, approximately 80 percent of the Indian population ascribe to Hinduism in their religious beliefs. This is followed by a 13 percent portion of the population identifying as Muslim, and a small minority – 2 percent – as Christian. The major religions of Buddhism and Hinduism were both started and spread in India, so it's not surprising the Hinduism has such a strong hold. However, the Constitution of India does maintain an open tolerance of religions, allowing a myriad of different belief systems to take hold, though they do so with smaller followings.

 Origins of Confucianism

Confucianism originated in approximately the 5th century BC in China. Many people debate whether it is technically a religion because it is not associated with any deities; however, it has been highly influential in shaping moral and social behaviors and norms in Chinese culture. Confucius himself was a scholar who was unable to attain an advisory in the courts of any officials. He instead spent his life traveling with a small group of followers and teaching the children of dignitaries. Confucianism came into being around the end of the warring states period in China at a time when there was a great amount of turmoil and change. As a result it tended to be highly conservative and emphasized the importance of respect and loyalty in a series of relationships, such as between father and son or between siblings.

 Religion in the United States

In the United States, Christianity is by a wide margin the most widely held belief system. Based on the US Census, approximately 80-85 percent of the US population holds to a Christian belief system. Other religions constitute only small portions of the total population. In fact, the second most common belief system is the reply of non-religious. This sector of the population has been growing with time, and now constitutes approximately 10-15 percent of the US population. Following non-religious individuals, the third largest religious group in the United States is Judaism, constituting just less than 2 percent of the population.

 General Population

Although populations had begun spreading across the earth in 10,000 BC, they were very different from populations today. First, the total population of the world is estimated to have been around 10 million (about 1.5 percent of today's world population). Communities were also characterized by a hunter-gatherer lifestyle. In other words, prior to this point in time the domestication of plants and beginning of agriculture had yet to occur. However, early evidence of domestic agriculture in some regions is dated to this approximate time period.

The exact timeline of human development is filled with holes and controversy. Determining an exact definition for the development of a human being is subjective and can as a result there is no universally accepted timeline for human development.

However, the majority of estimates place early humans in existence around 150-200 million years ago. Because the vast majority of early human fossils and discoveries have been made in Africa, it has come to be known as the cradle of the human race. Early humans were first found in the eastern part of the continent, and from there spread throughout the continent and into Asia, eventually reaching the farther lands of Europe and the Americas.

 Population Growth

Population growth is a complex measure because it can be affected by such as wide variety of factors. On the most basic level, a population will increase based on its birth rate and decrease based on its death or mortality rate. Rates of immigration and migration within the country will also have an impact on the population growth. One of the factors which complicates measurements of population increase is that specifically determining these rates can be difficult. Less developed countries simply do not have the resources or skills to do so, and even in more developed countries factors like illegal immigration, home births, unreported deaths and other factors make it extremely difficult to calculate exact changes in the population.

It can also be difficult to determine what it means for a country to have a certain growth rate. In a general sense, often the more developed a country is, the lower its birth rate will be. However, more developed countries often have a greater inflow of migrants, and a result their growth rates area not necessarily lower as a result.

Despite this fact, countries can be generally classified based on the population growth rates. Most countries with growth rates higher than 3 percent are in the less developed regions of Africa. Growth rates between 2-3 percent are also typical of these regions. A growth rate from 1-2 percent is typical of countries in South America, Australia, and the Middle East (from India to Turkey). Growth rates less than 1 percent are typical of Western Europe (e.g., Spain, France, and Britain), North American and China. Russia and Eastern Europe can have negative growth rates.

When it comes to migration, two important sets of factors provide motivation for people to change their location. These factors are push factors and pull factors (these are also referred to as push and pull forces). Forces which motivate people to want to leave a certain area are considered push factors because they essentially push a person out of the area. Push factors are typically the negative aspects of a region. They include problems such as droughts, famines, war, lack of jobs, overpopulation, discrimination, and anything else which motivates a person to leave an area.

On the other hand, pull factors are elements which motivate a person to want to be in another area. These are the benefits of a new area (beyond simply the absence of the push factors). Often push and pull forces work simultaneously to motivate a person to migrate. Examples of pull factors include better living standard, better pay, more political rights, being nearer to family, proximity to valuable natural resources, and an increased availability of work.

While a migrant is defined as a person who moves from one region to another by choice or plan, it is also important to consider those who move from one region to another because of forces outside their control. When a person is forced to leave their home they are referred to as a refugee. Refugees can be created as a result of political factors such as persecution or war, or even as a result of natural disasters such as hurricanes, tsunamis, tornados, floods, or others.

 Thomas Malthus

Thomas Malthus was an influential scholar who was born at the end of the seventeenth century. He theorized that because the world's resources increase at a consistent, or linear rate and the world's population grows exponentially (increasingly faster over time) that there will come a point when there will not be enough resources to support the world's growing population. This is demonstrated in the graph below.

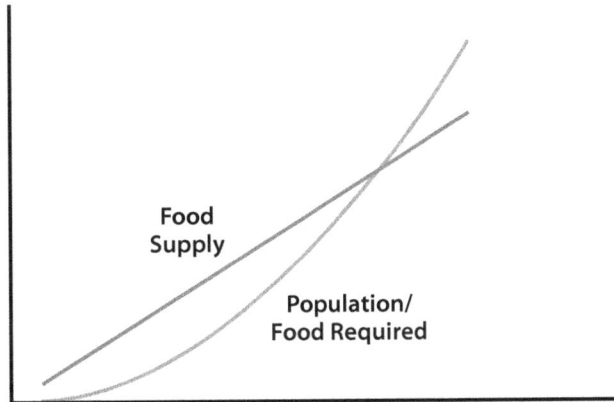

The result, according to Malthus, is that populations are naturally limited based on the availability of resources. His ideas influenced many important scientific minds, such as Charles Darwin in his development of the Theory of Evolution.

Dependency ratios are connected to Malthus' theories because they describe the relation between the people in a population who cannot work, (the dependents) divided by the number of people who can work. This is then multiplied by 100 to give a measure relative to every 100 people. Dependents are considered to be people younger than 15 or older than 64, while workers are anyone in between. Often, the more developed a country is, the lower its dependency ratio. Spain, for example, has a dependency ratio of about 45 people per 100 (in other words 45%). On the other hand Uganda has a dependency ratio of about 110 people per 100 (in other words 110%), meaning there are more dependents than there are workers.

Doubling Time

When studying populations, an important factor to consider is the doubling time. Although the physical size of a population should not be overlooked, the doubling time is important because it describes the rate at which that population is growing. Considering doubling time as opposed to or in conjunction with actual growth rate can be useful in creating a more easily conceptualized idea of how a population is growing. For example, a growth rate of 1 percent sounds fairly insignificant. However, the doubling time of such a population is approximately 70 years. This means that within the average person's lifetime the population will double in size. The doubling time of a population can be approximated with the equation $n=70/r$, where n is the doubling time and r is the growth rate.

Cultural Hearth

A cultural hearth is essentially the central location from which the innovations and aspects of a culture originate. Key cultural factors are first seen in these areas and eventually spread into surrounding areas. The earliest cultural hearths are those places in which the first urban centers developed as those centers grew and exerted influence over surrounding areas. The seven most important ancient cultural hearths are the Nile Valley or Indus Valley (i.e., the Egyptian civilization), Wei-Huang Valley (which is the root of the Chinese empire and culture), Ganges Valley (the cultural hearth of India), Mesopotamia, Mesoamerica (i.e., the Aztec civilization and others), West Africa, and Andean America (i.e., the Incan civilization).

 # Natural Resources

Resources, or naturally occurring materials necessary for human activity, affect the things that people do every day. The distribution of resources across the world is important because resources are necessary for food, fuel, clothing and shelter. Many of the factors affecting the world distribution of resources are geographic. For example, areas nearer the equator receive more sunlight; however, areas farther from the equator receive more precipitation and are therefore more suitable for growing crops. Another example is that minerals and metals are more commonly found near tectonic boundaries. These resources are springboards for economic development and urbanization, so the availability of resources greatly affects the development of a region. Some of the most important resources in the world today include water, soil, vegetation, metals, fuels, and animals.

Regions can be either resource-rich or resource-poor. If a region is resource-rich, this means that it has an abundance of a scarce natural resource. For example, Saudi Arabia is resource-rich in terms of petroleum. China is also considered resource rich because of its abundance of energy-producing materials, such as coal, iron, natural gas, uranium, population, and many excellent sites for hydropower. Oftentimes, the availability of resources allows a country to develop of thriving economy. This has been the case, for example, in the United States, China, Russia, and Canada, all of which are developed and resource-rich countries.

If a country is resource-poor this means that resources are scarce, and it must depend on other areas to provide resources. For example, while many African countries have an abundance of certain resources – such as diamonds in South Africa, or ivory in other areas – many have an extremely limited access to usable water or land space. Bahrain, Kenya, Saudi Arabia, Kuwait, Algeria, and Libya are some of the countries with the poorest water supply and quality.

Interestingly enough, however, while many African and Middle Eastern countries have little access to water, they are some of the most resource rich countries in the world in terms of minerals and fuels. This is called the resource paradox.

The resource paradox is that many of the most resource-rich countries in the world are some of the least developed countries. For example, Venezuela is considered to be one of the most resource rich countries, however the distribution of wealth gained from their resources is so concentrated that much of the population lives in poverty, making it a developing country. Because this paradox creates a situation where abundant resources do not lead to development and prosperity, it is necessary to specify whether countries are resource-rich or resource-poor and whether they are developed or undeveloped.

# Renewable Resources

An important factor to consider when it comes to natural resources is whether the resources are renewable or non-renewable. A resource is considered renewable if it is used or can feasibly be used at a rate which is sustainable (i.e., at a rate which can be maintained over time). When resources are used at a rate that both meets current needs and can be sustained it is referred to as sustainable development. A non-renewable resource, on the other hand, is a natural resource which cannot be generated indefinitely or sustainably. Some resources which are considered to be renewable include energy sources such as sunlight, tidal waves, wind, most animal populations, metals (which can be recycled and used many times as need be), and in some cases timber (because trees can be replanted).

Often of more important consideration, however, are non-renewable energy sources. Resources such as fossil fuels are considered non-renewable, even though they are generated naturally. This is because the rate at which they are replenished naturally is so much slower than the rate at which they must be used to meet current demands. In addition to fossil fuels such as coal, petroleum, and natural gas, another example of a non-renewable resource is endangered animals. Considering endangered animals also brings up another concern related to non-renewable energy sources: once they have been completely used (when a species goes extinct) it cannot be renewed.

# OPEC

One of the most influential intergovernmental organizations in the world today is OPEC. OPEC is the Organization of Petroleum Exporting Countries. The main purpose of OPEC is to protect the interests of the organization's members by ensuring that oil prices remain steady. In other words, OPEC is essentially an international cartel of oil-exporting countries which works to manipulate the price and availability of oil to the best benefit of members. OPEC was originally formed in the 1960's by five countries - Iran, Iraq, Kuwait, Saudi Arabia, and Venezuela. Since that time these five founding countries have been joined by the United Arab Emirates, Algeria, Nigeria, Angola, and Gabon.

# Cultures and Crop Bases

In today's market, plants and ingredients can be transported across the world, creating access to a variety of flavors and meals. However, this has not always been the case. The domestication of plants for use as a food source is a process that has occurred slowly over the course of human development. As early nomadic groups learned to domesticate plants, and farms became possible, the gradual shift in living patterns from hunter-gatherer to small communities began to occur.

Cultures across the world all evolved different crop bases from which to form their diets. In North America, domestication of plant species began as early as 5000 BC through two main sources. First, the plants native to Mesoamerica – i.e., squash, corn (maize), and beans – spread north and eventually east, becoming important staples in the diets of Native Americans. However, the early residents of eastern North America can also be credited with the domestication of various plants. These include marshelder, chenopod, squash, and sunflower.

The rough, uneven terrain and difficult climate of Mediterranean regions gave rise to unique plant domestication. Because of the uneven terrain, farming is highly labor intensive. Regardless of this fact, the domestication of cereals and grains (e.g., barley and wheat) constitutes nearly half of the agriculture. The raising of orchards is also a central feature of Mediterranean agriculture. The climate of the region is characterized by rain in the winter and long periods of summer drought. As a result, crops which are typical of Mediterranean agriculture include tough, thick-skinned crops which can flourish in the arid temperatures. For example, citrus, dates, figs, olives, and grapes are all important in Mediterranean agriculture.

 Domestication of Animals

Historically speaking, next to the cultivation of agriculture (also known as the domestication of plants or agriculture) the domestication of animals was one of the most important developments in the progression of human civilizations. The uses associated with domestication of animals come in a number of different forms. Firstly, cultivating animals as a food source is an important form of domestication. While hunter/gatherer populations subsisted on hunted beasts, cultivating animals such as pigs, chickens, cows, llamas, and others as the geographic location allowed was an important element of civilization.

Another factor in the domestication of animals is the use of beasts of burden. Beasts of burden are large load-bearing animals. Populations in areas of the world with beasts of burden were able to harness the strength and other attributes of these animals to be more productive. While the domestication of animals was an important factor in the progression of civilizations, it is by no means a widespread phenomenon. Of the millions of known species on the earth, a rare few have been and are suitable to domestic use by humans. In fact, fewer than 30 species have been domesticated, including dogs, sheep, cattle, goats, chickens, donkeys, bees, camels, horses, and others.

While people most often think of some animals in the context of pests that cause problems for human populations, in many cases they can be useful or even central to the survival of populations. One such example of this is the mongoose. A mongoose appears similar to weasel, and they are found in Africa, and in some areas of the Middle East (e.g., they are known for being found in India, Pakistan, and Egypt).

The important use of the mongoose is its diet. They are known for fighting, killing, and eating many species of venomous snakes, making them a useful protective animal in these areas. Their diet also includes the occasional crocodile egg and carrion. The mongoose is also an integral part of the culture in the region as they are often used by snake charmers in staged fights for show and various other functions (however, this is becoming less common due to the actions of animal rights groups). The serve the same function as a farmer who keeps a cat in the barn to rid it of mice.

Urbanization

In today's society it is difficult to imagine a world without cities; however, at the beginning of the 19th century fewer than one in ten individuals lived in a city. Furthermore, those cities were far smaller than the cities that exist today. Since the onset of the industrial revolution both the size and number of cities has increased as the world has faced the process of urbanization. Now, on a worldwide scale over half of the population resides in urban areas. Statistics are even higher within the United States where the urban population is about 80 percent.

Going back to urbanization in its earliest stages, the development of the city can be attributed to five independent urban centers which are referred to as urban hearths. The first cities and urban centers can be traced to Mesopotamia as early as 3500 BC. This area, now better known as the Fertile Crescent is referred to as the first urban hearth.

The second urban hearth is the Nile River Valley of Egypt, in which early cities are dated to have begun forming shortly afterwards in 3200 BC. The third urban hearth is the Indus River Valley in India. Cities here are believed to have begun forming around 2200 BC. The fourth urban hearth is attributed to China. More specifically it is between the Huang He and Wei rivers, with cities dating to approximately 1500 BC.

The final urban hearth is Mesoamerica, where significant civilizations began to form much later, around 200 BC. The development of these five cultural hearths is often referred to as the first urban revolution. This is the first period in history in which human populations began to settle into cities, and it marks an important era of human development.

In more modern times, urbanization trends can be directly correlated with industrialization patterns. While the first urban revolution is characterized by the innovation of the city, modern urbanization is characterized by the development of much larger, industrialized, urban centers. Due to the many innovations, and the fact that prior to the industrial revolution many of the world's largest cities were in Britain, it was a major center of urbanization. Within mainland Europe, one of the primary locations for this urbanization was the heavy industrial sector of Germany known as the Rhine Ruhr Valley, which is approximately on the border between Germany and France. As industrialization spread throughout Europe and into the United States, urbanization followed.

Urban Development of North American Cities

The structure of a city is all about access. Businesses want to be as accessible as possible, and individuals want easy access to all of the commodities, goods, and services that they want and need. This drive for accessibility determines the urban layout. In North American cities the lowest population density is always at the center of a city. While this may seem counterintuitive, it is actually quite logical. The reason that the population density is lowest at the center is because this area is occupied by primarily businesses and commercial centers, rather than residences (i.e., it is the CBD).

Just outside this area of low population density, is where the greatest population density is because people wish to be close to their work, shopping locations, and other conveniences. From this ring of dense population, the population density gradually decreases farther out from the CBD.

Central Place Theory

The central place theory was developed in the early 1990s by Walter Christaller as an explanation of urban development. Christaller noticed that the largest cities in an area tended to be fairly equally distributed. He referred to these major urban centers as Central Places. The farther off areas which travel to the central place are referred to as hinterlands.

For each central place there is a specific associated range and threshold. The threshold is the minimum amount of area that a city needs to have its economy supported. For example, the distance that people must be willing to travel to buy goods in order for a company to make sufficient profit to stay in operation. The range is the actual distance that people are willing to travel in order to gain the service that a center offers. When the range is greater than the threshold then the center will flourish and grow. However, if the threshold is greater than the range it will flounder because it is will not be able to support itself. Because not everyone with be within the range for a certain central place, multiple central places will spring up, all of which are approximately equal distances from each other. Christaller theorized a hexagonal model to model the placement of central places across the map (in other words, the ranges take a hexagonal shape so that no area is left without access to a central place).

Urban Hierarchy

As an area becomes increasingly urbanized, different cities will often develop different functions and capacities in relation to each other. The ranking of different urban centers is referred to as an urban hierarchy. There are four orders or ranks within the urban hierarchy. A first order town is a smaller, less densely populated area. These towns provide only the minimum accommodations (e.g., food, clothing, etc.) for their inhabitants. Service-oriented or specialized markets do not thrive in first order towns because they are typically less populated and are more oriented towards self-sufficiency. First order centers are also often referred to as hamlets.

A second order urban center, occasionally referred to as a village, will provide a more specialized selection of services. Second order centers are somewhat more populous and are spaced farther apart from each other than are first order centers. The influence of a second order center may extend to a number of first order centers which will travel to them for services. For example, whereas a first order center may have a small grocery store, individuals may travel to a nearby second-order center for somewhat more specialized products like gas, movies, or a trip to a restaurant.

A third order and fourth order urban centers are even larger than a second order centers, and will offer an even wider variety of goods and services. Third order centers are also referred to as towns, and fourth order centers as cities. In terms of size, fourth order centers will have a central city area surrounded by suburbs, while a third order center will not be large enough to classify as suburbs. As you move up the urban hierarchy (i.e., from first order to second, or from second to third, etc.) the centers become both larger and spread farther apart. This is because people will be willing to travel farther to reach the services which they offer.

Primate City

A primate city is a city that is twice the size of the next largest city in a nation. Primate cities tend to be the centers of economy, politics, and culture for the states in which they reside simply because they encompass such a large portion of the population. Primate cities are also typically important in the development and urbanization of the state. Some examples of primate cities today include Paris (seven times larger than Marseilles, France's second largest city), London (seven times larger than the UK's second largest city, Birmingham), and Mexico City (five times larger than Guadalajara).

Urban Sprawl

Urban sprawl is when suburbs and large cities grow so much that they become one large rambling city. This is because the central city develops as a main center of business, filling with offices, company headquarters, strip malls, restaurants, parking structures, and other types of businesses. This leaves less and less room for housing, forcing people to relocate outside the central city area, and commute into the city for work. Urban sprawl is an uncontrolled and unplanned expansion of an urban area. Because of the environmental impact, along with increased infrastructure costs, urban sprawl is often looked on negatively.

Urban Heat Island

An urban heat island can most simply be described as a "hot spot" on the surface of the earth that is caused by urbanization. That is, large cities have a tendency to have slightly higher temperatures than the suburban and rural areas that surround them. There are a number of different causes of urban heat islands. One cause of urban heat islands is the removal of vegetation. Rural areas tend to be covered in vegetation which both absorbs heat, and helps the land retain moisture (absorbing additional heat). As an area becomes more urbanized, the vegetation is replaced by buildings and other structures, making the land increasingly drier and less open.

A second cause of urban heat islands is feedback from the buildings and structures themselves. Asphalt, cement, brick, and buildings in general all absorb and hold heat from the sun, heating to as much as 50 degrees warmer than the surrounding air temperature. As these things heat up, they will contribute to raising air temperatures along with the heat from the sun. A third cause of urban heat islands is as a result of the higher levels of greenhouse gases which hold in the heat more so than in the surrounding areas.

 Metropolis and Megalopolis

A metropolitan area, or metropolis, is basically a large city. A metropolis includes the main city and any surrounding suburban areas. Generally, a metropolis has at least 50,000 people in the main city with more in the surrounding areas. Paris and New York are both metropolitan areas. Tokyo is considered the largest metropolitan area in the world. When two or more metropolitan areas that are near each other and both grow to the extent that their boundaries overlap it is called a megalopolis. A megalopolis is characterized by dense population, high levels of urbanization, and a thriving economy.

In the United States there are a number of important megalopolis regions. Most of these regions are located in the eastern half of the country, although there are some in the western half. For example, one important west-coast megalopolis is referred to as the Northern California megalopolis. This megalopolis comprises the major cities of Fresno, Reno, Sacramento, San Francisco, and others in the surrounding area.

The largest megalopolis areas in the country, however, are found farther east. For example, the area surrounding the Great Lakes is one of large megalopolis areas in the United States. This megalopolis supports a population of well over 50 million, and its span includes major cities such as Chicago, Detroit, Pittsburgh, Cincinnati, Buffalo, Montreal, Toronto and others. One of the most famous megalopolis areas in the United States is referred to as the Northeast megalopolis, or more simply as BosNyWash. This megalopolis supports a similarly large population, and spans the three major cities of Boston, New York, and Washington DC. It is also comprised of the major cities of Baltimore, Philadelphia, Hartford, and others.

Friedman's Model of Regional Development

John Friedman developed a Model of Regional Development which essentially translates the core-periphery model to a regional or even city-wide level. Friedman's model divides regions into four different stages based on levels of development and behaviors. Stage 1 is also referred to as the pre-industrial stage. In this stage, the region eventually becoming the core is a small, localized region with its own isolated economy. There is little mobility and there is little trade or interaction with outside entities.

Stage 2 is also referred to as the transitional stage. This stage is characterized by a concentration of the economy on the core region. Essentially, this region begins to industrialize, and resources begin to concentrate there to allow growth and development. As resources concentrate, the core begins to expand to include upward transitional areas or resource frontiers. These areas are essentially the semi-periphery to the core. They have access to resources needed by the expanded core, and therefore reap positive benefits from proximity to it. However, the process also results in the creation of downward transition areas. These areas reap negative effects from the growth of the periphery as populations move inward and the economy of the areas suffer as a result.

In Stage 3, or the industrial stage, other urban centers begin to grow and expand through trade with the original core region. Essentially, the concentration of the economy lessens as some of the periphery settlements are able to build up their own economies (the core economy is still strong, the wealth and prosperity just begins to spread as other settlements industrialize). This is caused by increasing prosperity and need as the core cannot support its own growth due to land and labor needs as it expands.

Finally, Stage 4, or the post-industrial stage, is characterized by an integration of the different economic centers to create a core region with a specialized and functioning economy. A strong infrastructure will exist between the various core settlements that reduce the regional inequalities. This works to the benefit of the many core and periphery areas, and results in economic prosperity.

 # *Core-Periphery Model*

One popular view of the world structure is the Core-Periphery model. According to this model, the world can be divided into core regions and periphery regions. The model essentially describes the phenomenon that as the world grows more prosperous and industrial on a cumulative basis, the improvements in technology and trade are enjoyed by a few core regions. This is evidenced by that fact that the vast majority of the global annual income is shared by a small percentage of the world population (approximately 15 percent). This disparity is caused initially by a more efficient use and availability of resources, but eventually becomes a pattern caused by exploitation or ignorance on the part of core countries. In other words, the core countries build their economies legitimately, but then the periphery countries are so far behind in terms of development that they cannot attain the same levels easily.

The core is commonly accepted to consist of Europe, the United States, Canada, Australia, Japan, and Israel (and a few others to a lesser degree). These countries drive the majority of innovation and societal improvements. In addition they are characterized by high-functioning infrastructures, high levels of globalization, and access to health services.

The periphery is basically the rest of the world. Countries in Africa, South America, Asia, and Russia are all considered to be a part of the periphery. These countries do not enjoy the benefits of infrastructure, communication, and heath care enjoyed by the rich core. In fact, they are characterized by low levels of development (resulting in high population growth), and low living conditions.

There are many places on earth where the interactions caused by proximity between the core and the periphery result in clear conflict. For example, the fence which is continually being built between Mexico and the United States is one such area of conflict. This is an effort to stop the illegal immigration of individuals of the periphery, Mexico, to the core, the United States. A second example is the forced demilitarization of the border between North and South Korea to reduce conflict (North Korea is considered periphery, whereas South Korea is generally considered to be a part of the core).

Developing Countries

In order to compare various countries across the world there are a number of terms which are used. Countries can be classified as developed, underdeveloped, or developing. While these terms are relative to a certain extent, the UN has created a quantitative measure called the Human Development Index (HDI) to make comparison more feasible. A country is considered developed, or is considered a More Developed Country (MDC), if it has a high level of economic developed and a high HDI. The HDI measure is essentially a measure of living standards and quality in a country. It takes into account a number of factors such as life expectancy, education, schooling, and national income. In addition to high living standards and a stable economy, developed countries are also characterized by good infrastructure, stable and typically smaller populations, and a general security.

In contrast to developed countries, undeveloped countries have low HDI scores and may have highly unstable or dysfunctional economies. Underdeveloped countries are also referred to as Less or Least Developed Countries (LDC's). These countries are characterized by very poor living conditions. Disease and poverty may be rampant, along with characteristically low incomes and low levels of literacy and education. In addition, LDC's tend to have high birth rates (often coupled with a very high infant mortality), which leads to higher overall populations. LDC's are also often characterized by poor infrastructure, few job opportunities, and corrupt or ineffective governments.

Countries which are in between the status of LDC and MDC are referred to as developing countries. These countries can be hard to classify because they are essentially a mix of the characteristics of the two statuses. They have mid-range HDI scores, and are making steps towards increased living standards and stabilized economies. In terms of worldwide development, the general distribution of developed and underdeveloped countries is clustered around the globe. The majority of the world's MDCs are in North America and Europe. In contrast, the majority of LDC's are located in rural regions of Africa, along with some in South America and Asia. The developing countries of the world comprise the more developed sectors of these three continents. For example, MDC's include the United States, Switzerland, Britain, and France. LDC's include Cambodia, Laos, Congo, and Kenya. Finally, examples of developing countries include Venezuela, Thailand, and South Africa.

Wallerstein's World Systems Theory

One notable cultural geographer is Immanuel Wallerstein. Wallerstein is known for his work in developing World Systems Theory. This theory is a framework describing the development of the modern world, and describes the stages that occurred in making the world what it is today. Wallerstein argued that in order to understand the current economic and political scene, it was necessary to follow the social and economic development throughout history. He considered the world to have become essentially one large capitalist market, ruled by competition and the availability of goods.

Wallerstein divided the world into three different types of states: core, semi-periphery, and periphery. Peripheral areas are the underdeveloped (or at the very least, least developed) states. Due to their disadvantage in terms of development and industrialization they are exploited as a source of cheap labor and resources. The semi-peripheral areas are the "in between" areas.

They lack the complexity and full urbanization of the core regions, but may have a thriving marketing sector and may participate in the exploitation of the periphery. Finally, the core regions are the most developed, urbanized, and industrialized states. They are advantaged geographically, educationally, militarily, and in other important ways.

Wallerstein identified four stages through which the world economy progressed in its development. Stages one and two describe the world in the 16th and 17th centuries. During this time European governments began to centralize and bureaucratize. They built up armies to solidify their power and began establishing long-distance trade patterns to build their economies.

Stages three and four describe the world after the onset of the 18th century. These stages are characterized by a shifting from an agricultural-based economy to an industrialized economy. The core, European states shifted their focus from the trade of agricultural products (i.e., tea, spices, tobacco, sugar, etc.) to manufactured products. This spurred the exploitation of the peripheral states to gain access to labor and especially raw materials necessary to allow this industrialization.

 # Economic Systems

The term economic system refers to the structure of elements within an economy. In other words, how goods are made, transported, and traded between members of populations. There are four basic economic systems: subsistence, commercial, planned, and mixed. Subsistence, or traditional, economic systems are those in which individuals are concerned only with generating enough to live on (i.e., enough for subsistence). These are the most historically common economic systems, involving isolated groups of individuals which farm for the overwhelming majority of their goods, sew their own clothes, and so forth. These types of economic systems have very small markets because they are not geared towards producing goods to trade. When trade is necessary, a barter system is used rather than a formal system of money.

The second economic system, the commercial system, often replaces such traditional systems. Commercial economic systems are also referred to as capitalist systems or market systems. Commercial systems are characterized by markets which change and fluctuate based on the forces of supply and demand. They are based on and monitored by the fluctuations in market prices. Decisions about what to produce are made based on the demand, availability, and cost-effectiveness of producing them. Decisions on transportation additionally consider these factors. As a result, this type of system relies heavily on competition and trade to determining its structure and function.

The third type of economic system is the planned economic system. This is also referred to as the socialist or centrally planned economic system. This type of system derives its structure solely from the decision of a central power (i.e., government) of some sort. This type of structure describes that of socialist or communist countries. For example, the former Soviet Union, Cuba, and China are all examples of planned economic systems.

The final type of economic system is the mixed economic system. This type of system combines elements of both commercial and planned systems. That is, the market is able to operate freely to a great degree, but the government can intervene in some respects. For example, taxes, subsidies, laws about monopolies, and other factors. The United States economy, for example, would most correctly be described under this category.

Rostow's Stages of Development

Another notable cultural geographer is Walt Whitman Rostow. Rostow developed a model of economic development which traces the development of economies through five major stages. Rostow's model serves as both a description of a pattern seen in the economic development of many countries, and as a model to be followed for LDC's hoping to achieve increased economic development. A fundamental concept of Rostow's model is the investment in capital for later production and therefore later benefit.

Rostow's first stage is Traditional Society. The traditional society is essentially the most primitive type of society. These societies are characterized by low levels of development and urbanization. Economies at this point could be characterized by either subsistence-level function or hunter/gatherer techniques. Agricultural products compose the majority of the economic product, and when trade occurs a simple barter system is used. Traditional societies are additionally characterized by extremely low levels of social and economic mobility. That is, people are essentially "stuck" where they are in terms of economic status, both during their lives and intergenerationally.

The second stage Rostow identified is the Transitional Stage (also referred to as Preconditions for Take-Off). In this stage, the market begins its transition to an industrial market. Although industrialization is not widespread at this point, people begin to invest in capital and accumulate raw materials. A small degree of the capacity for individual mobility develops, and the market begins to specialize. Further, the infrastructure increases and improves, which paves the way for later industrialization and development to occur.

The third stage identified by Rostow is referred to as Take Off. It is in this stage that full industrialization occurs. A few manufacturing industries emerge and grow (one common take off industry being textiles). This stage is also characterized by surplus. In other words, for the first time the market is really producing enough both for local consumption and for exportation and trade.

The fourth stage of Rostow's stages of development is Drive to Maturity. This stage refers to the diversification process which must occur for an economy to become truly stable. Manufacturing begins to focus on the production of consumer goods. While the Take Off stage is characterized by the rise of a few primal manufacturing sectors, during the Drive to Maturity stage the economy becomes increasingly self-sufficient and industrial. There is large-scale attention paid to both the investment in human and social capital (education, research, technology, etc.) and to the development of adequate infrastructure to serve the growing market.

The fifth and final stage is the Age of Mass Consumption. This stage characterizes the developed, core regions of the world today. Markets are highly industrialized and focused on providing specialized consumer goods to the general public, which at this point has progressed to a stage in which they have the disposable income to support the market production. A strong service sector also emerges.

Clark's Sector Model

According to economist Colin Clark, there are four different sectors of an economy, and as a community develops over time there will be a different emphasis placed in each of these different sectors. The four sectors are referred to as primary, secondary, tertiary, and quaternary activities. Primary activities are those which involve the direct extraction and handling of raw materials. Mining, hunting, farming, fishing, and other such activities all qualify as primary sector activities.

Secondary activities are those which involve manufacturing and construction activities. The tertiary sector of the economy is the service sector. Tertiary sector activities include education, financial services, health care, and others. Finally, the quaternary sector of the economy is the information or intellectual sector of the economy. Quaternary activities include information gathering and management.

Countries whose economies are focused around lower sector activities (i.e., primary sector activities) tend to be far less developed and prosperous than those involved with higher level activities. Countries whose economies are primarily in the primary sector correlate to periphery or pre-industrial societies. This isn't to say that these economies only have primary activities. Rather, they have very low levels of secondary and tertiary activities if they do exist.

Countries with economies dominated by secondary activities tend to be the transitional countries in terms of development. They have little agricultural product, but have mid-range incomes and living standards. Therefore, countries with economies that are centered in mainly secondary sector activities tend to be the industrializing or semi-periphery countries in society. Typically, the presence of tertiary sector activities is greater at this stage of development than for a primary sector economy; however, the majority of the capital will be dedicated to secondary sector activities, and the amount of primary activities will have declined.

Economies which have progressed to include tertiary sector activities tend to be the more highly developed countries, and have higher living standards and incomes. These economies will have lower levels of primary and secondary sector activities, rather obtaining goods through trade with less developed regions. Further, it is at this point that the quaternary sector activities are able to emerge, working alongside the tertiary sector activities.

 # *Hoyt's Sector Model*

The Hoyt model, or sector model was created by Hoyt as a model of urban development. Instead of concentric circles or adjacent hexagons, Hoyt believed that cities developed according to different sectors, which occupied wedges moving out from the center of the city. Hoyt believed that at the center of an urban area was a circular sector called the central business district (CBD). This area is the most conveniently and centrally located, and as a result land prices and congestion is high.

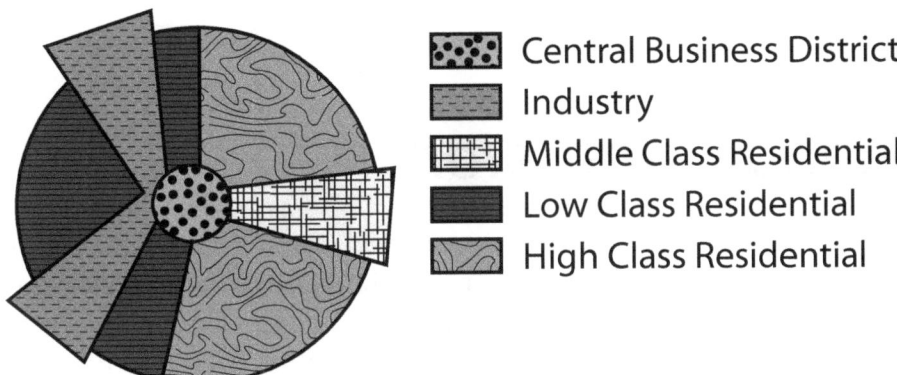

Central Business District
Industry
Middle Class Residential
Low Class Residential
High Class Residential

Therefore, it is primarily businesses and commercial shops that occupy this area. Branching off in two wedges from the central business district tis the industry sector. This sector is the older industries that were started before the central business district development. Around these wedges is the low class housing (because typically few people want to live in old industrial areas). Opposite the industrial wedges will be the middle class housing, surrounded by high class housing.

 # *Burgess/Concentric Zone Model*

Another model of urban development is known as the concentric zone model. This model was proposed by E.W. Burgess, and it begins with a central business district at the center of the urban area. This CBD is then surrounded by outward radiating concentric zones each of which describes a certain type of industry or residence it has developed as the city grows. Just outside the CBD is the industrial sector, followed by the low class, middle class, and finally suburban housing.

 Diffusion

In science, diffusion refers to the process through which something spreads or fills a space. Such as a scent spreading to fill a room, or food coloring spreading throughout a liquid. In geography, the term has similar connotations, but in terms of information. Diffusion is the process by which information, technology, diseases, and innovations spread from their origin, or hearth, to other areas. There are many different types of diffusion, the most important of which are relocation diffusion and spatial diffusion, which occurs in three different ways: hierarchical diffusion, contagious diffusion, and stimulus diffusion.

 Relocation Diffusion

Relocation diffusion is when things spread through the physical movement of individuals. For example, diseases spread through relocation diffusion because they require that people physically move to spread them. Throughout history relocation diffusion was the most common, and in some cases the only way for diffusion to occur. People would take with them their cultures and practices when they would migrate from one place to another. However, as communication technology improves, other forms of diffusion have become both possible and more common.

 Spacial Diffusion

Spatial diffusion is the spread of ideas and information in a snowballing process; i.e., from place to place to place, etc. It involves moving outward from a specific location. The three different types of expansion diffusion are hierarchical diffusion, contagious diffusion, and stimulus diffusion.

Hierarchical Diffusion

Hierarchical diffusion occurs when diffusion happens through the individuals of authority in a culture or population. For example, styles may leek down and change as nobles or important governmental leaders come to power with different styles. However, hierarchical diffusion need not be spread through individuals of political authority. Another example is that music styles can be altered and changed as popular musicians in a certain genre alter their style, and others change to be similar to them.

Contagious Diffusion

Contagious or expansion diffusion is a rapid, widespread diffusion of a characteristic throughout a population. Whereas hierarchical diffusion spreads through a specific downward hierarchy, and is a slower and more evolutionary process, contagious diffusion can be almost instantaneous. For example, information that is placed on the internet spreads throughout the population as quickly as people begin to view it. It is sporadic and quick, but can still be said to spread outward from a specific idea.

Stimulus Diffusion

Stimulus diffusion is the spread of a principle even when a characteristic itself doesn't diffuse, but its underlying principle does diffuse. For example, a person could put forth the idea of cutting down on pollution by using cars that ran on water instead of gas, but instead people decided that they would just be more conscious of their fuel consumption. If this idea were to become widespread and people began using more fuel-efficient cars, and cutting down pollution in other ways, it would be an example of stimulus diffusion. The original idea stimulated a change, even though it did not diffuse through the population itself.

Demographic Transition Model

The demographic transition model was developed by an American demographer Warren Thompson. The model describes a transition by countries from a state of high birth and death rates to low birth and death rates as they become increasingly developed. There are five stages in the demographic transition model.

The first stage of the demographic transition model characterizes pre-industrial societies. These societies have high birth (infant mortality) and death rates that are approximately in balance. This is typically a result of poor medical and hygiene practices, so that individuals have shorter life spans and higher infant mortality. As a result populations are kept fairly low.

The second stage of the demographic transition model characterizes developing or urbanizing societies. These societies have a rapid increase in hygienic practices. Populations also have an increased grasp of their food supplies. As a result, general health of the population increases and they have longer life expectancy and less disease.

Therefore, developing societies are characterized by low/declining death rates, coupled with the still-high birth rates. This imbalance results in population growth.

The third stage of the demographic transition model characterizes countries which are essentially transitioning from developing to developed societies. The countries in this stage are also referred to as mature industrial societies. At this stage in the demographic transition birth rates begin to fall. This occurs for a number of reasons, including increased awareness of contraceptive methods, increased education for women, urbanization, and increased access to medical technology. Due to the holding low death rates, the decrease in birth rates allows the population to begin leveling off at a now higher level than previously.

The fourth stage of the demographic transition model characterizes developed or post-industrial countries. At this point, both the birth rates and the death rates are at low levels, resulting in relatively stable population. However, unlike the first stage in which the population is held at a relatively low level, it is now maintained at a relatively high level. In some cases the birth rate may even drop below maintenance level, causing a small amount of population shrinkage (this occurred in Japan, Germany, and Italy).

Energy Consumption

One common indicator used to determine the economic development of a region is to look at the per capita energy consumption for commercial uses. The higher the per capita energy consumption is, the more developed a region is considered to be. This is because the use of technology and access to electricity is higher in consumer-oriented, developed markets, than it is in the more rural and poor underdeveloped regions. On average, energy consumption in developed regions is ten times that of less developed regions. For example, the world average energy consumption is approximately 300 watts per person. This is a mere 5 percent of the average 5900 watts per person in the developed country of Iceland. Even in the United States energy use is more than quadruple the world average, coming in at nearly 1400 watts per person. These amounts dwarf the energy use values in less economically developed regions such as Afghanistan and Rwanda, both of which average 1 watt per person, or even North Korea which falls short of 100 watts per person.

In developed countries the need for making power is becoming more and more important. One of the more controversial ways of producing that power is with a nuclear power plant.

Many of the objections that people have to nuclear plants are cosmetic rather than scientific. For this reason, countries may often choose to have nuclear plants in more rural and isolated areas rather than in urban areas. For example, whether as a result of misinformation or fears, the presence of nuclear plants often makes property values decline. Therefore, placing them in rural areas circumnavigates this issue to a large degree. Worries about the effects of waste, spills, and complications are further alleviated as plants are moved to more rural areas where there are fewer people, and there is more space.

Carl O. Sauer

One famous geographer who worked more recently is Carl O. Sauer. Sauer rejected the popular idea of environmental determinism (that environments make people who they are), and rather promoted the process of studying the interactions between environments and history; i.e., how the landscape affects a population over time. One of his early works, entitled "The Morphology of a Landscape," was instrumental in developing and popularizing the idea of cultural landscapes. Sauer felt strongly that the domestication of plants and animals from specific historical hearths was essential to understanding geography and the development of human populations.

Richard Hartshorne

Another important geographer of recent note is named Richard Hartshorne. Hartshorne's most famous work was entitled "The Nature of Geography." In his book, Hartshorne discussed the application and purpose of geography extensively. Much of Hartshorne's theory was pulled from German geographers. Hartshorne argued that the study of geography should be limited to a purely spatial perspective, rather than incorporating various other elements.

Centripetal and Centrifugal Forces

Two of the overarching forces discussed in terms of political geography are centrifugal and centripetal forces. These two forces operate in opposition to each other to either create or destroy unity in a given area. Centripetal forces are the forces which work to bind a country together. Any sort of unifying factor, whether cultural, geographic, political, or otherwise which brings people together is considered a centripetal force. For example, shared language, religion, education, history, and values are all considered to be centripetal forces in political geography.

In contrast, centrifugal forces in political geography are elements which tear unity apart. The presence of multiple languages and religions, for example, is an increasingly common centrifugal force in the world today. Many African populations are characterized by hundreds of different tribal languages and religious structures. Even in more developed regions there are centrifugal forces caused by language. One particularly powerful example is the presence of Basque populations in Spain. The Basque language has become a bit of a mystery to linguists, who are unable to trace it to any other language family or line. Rather, it seems to have developed distinctly. Because the Basque people inhabit their own secluded region of the country, they have effectively remained distinct from the mainstream Spanish population throughout history. Hence, the presence of the Basques in Spain is an example of a centrifugal force.

Language is also a relevant centrifugal force in Canada. Because of Canada's large size, some areas develop much more similarly to United States populations (in terms of culture, language, etc.) than they do with other Canadian populations. For example, consider the Quebecois. A Quebecois is essentially a resident of the province of Quebec, many of whom consider themselves to be French Canadians. Multiple times the province of Quebec has attempted to secede from Canada due to their strong affiliation with the French language and culture, which they feel distinguishes them as a separate nation from the rest of the country. Hence, language again becomes an important centrifugal force.

Unique political situations or factors can also cause centrifugal forces to arise. One important example of this in the world today is the presence of the Palestinian people in Lebanon. In the mid-20th century, the Arab-Israeli War caused the flight of massive numbers of Palestinian refugee into Lebanon. The resulting population of more than 250 thousand Palestinian refugees within the state of Lebanon has created a unique and tense political situation. The Palestinian refugees are denied citizenship and the right to work in over 25 different fields. Their political and economic standings are restricted and insufficient. The Palestinian people are essentially isolated from the remainder of the population; therefore, the political and economic discrimination is an example of a centrifugal force.

 Colonies and Imperialism

An important aspect which made the world what it is today is the practice of imperialism and colonialism by European nations throughout the previous centuries. Colonialism refers to situations in which a particular country settles in another land and thereby gains control over it. For example, North America was colonized by various European nations – France colonized what is now Canada and Britain colonized what is now the United States. The important thing to remember of colonization is that it involves direct implantation by the dominant country. If a country is colony then from a political standpoint they are subject to the laws and politics of the dominant country.

Closely related to the idea of colonization is the idea of imperialism. Stated most simply, when a country takes control of another region that is in a different area, it is referred to as imperialism. The two main differences between colonization and imperialism are that rather than settling an area or moving into it, as with colonization, imperialism typically involves taking control of an already populated area. A colony follows the laws and political movements of the dominant country, but with imperialism the dominant country may simply take control of the already existing political structure in the country. When countries maintain control of colonies in different areas of the world it is imperialism.

One clear examples of European imperialism is the state of Africa during the 1900's. Essentially, all of the major European nations of the time met together and divided the continent amongst themselves into different areas of control. As a result, essentially all African nations were at one point a colony of a European nation. More modern examples of colonies include the Virgin Islands (which were colonies of Great Britain), or Guam and Puerto Rico (which are colonies or commonwealths of the United States).

Expansionism

Expansionism is the idea that economic growth depends on a country's ability to grow and expand and increase its sphere of influence. Although a belief in this policy was manifested by many European countries throughout history in the form of imperialism, the United States actually pushed against it until the turn of the 20th century. For example, the early policy of the United States was to stay out of European affairs and the affairs of neighboring countries.

However, as forces of globalization began to ensue with the onset of World Wars I and II, expansionism became a much more prevalent concept. The United States began attempting to extend its influence to countries such as Cuba and Panama. In addition, the cold war was essentially a war of expansionism. The communist countries were attempting to gain additional followers, and the United States feared this because it gave them increased economic control.

Borders and Country Shapes

Countries come in all different shapes and sizes based on the historical developments that formed them. While some nations in history managed to expand their influence over great distances (e.g., the Roman and British Empires), such large-scale control has rarely been maintained over time due to the many difficulties which arise. The most efficient shape for a country is a small, compact, roughly round shape.

This allows for the government to maintain control much more easily, and ensures that the interests of the population as a whole are in unison. One reason why this is the case is because it avoids the problem of different regions forming with unique interests. Small, compact countries also tend to be easier to govern because there are fewer problems of infrastructure. For example, with the Roman Empire a large factor in the eventual collapse was an inability to communicate effectively with distant parts of the empire.

Gerrymandering

One interesting application of using geography in today's world that shows the importance of location is referred to as gerrymandering. Gerrymandering is an attempt to establish a political advantage for a particular candidate or individual by drawing voting districts to be most advantageous. For example, by setting voting districts to ensure that a certain number of areas it will have the effect of manipulating the majority votes for or against incumbent officials or for or against certain laws. Typically, gerrymandering has a negative connotation as a way to "game" the system.

Burkina Faso

Burkina Faso is a small country in Africa which is approximately the size of the state of Colorado (i.e., approximately 105 square miles or 275 square kilometers). It is bordered to the south by Ghana, to the east by Niger, and to the north and west by Mali. The official language of Burkina Faso is French, and over half of the population is Muslim. Burkina Faso declared its independence from France not long ago in 1960, and have since that time had only one ruler (he has won in every election). Because it is so small and lacks many natural resources, there are few economic prospects.

# *Russia*

Throughout the years there have been many empires which prided themselves on the fact that the sun never set on their empire – Britain and Rome being two of the most notable. Surprisingly, this can also be said of Russia. When the sun is setting in the western metropolis St. Petersburg, the sun is already rising on its pacific shores. Russia spans a massive 17.1 million kilometers of area. This makes it nearly double the size of the United States (1.8 to be more precise), and is half the size of the entire continent of Africa. To cross the country by plane would take around 10 hours. By train, the trek takes nearly a week.

# Unique South American Countries

The geography of South America is actually quite unique. There are twelve independent states in South America, in addition to a number of dependent territories. While many countries, such as Chile and Brazil, have a massive amount of coastal space, two of the twelve independent states in South America are entirely landlocked. They are Paraguay and Bolivia, giving these two states cultural aspects unique to them amongst many South American countries.

# Language Families

The broadest classification system used when considering languages is the classification into language families. Language families classify different languages based on their historical developments. The largest branch of language families are referred to as Indo-European languages.

The languages included in the Indo-European language family include languages which developed in Europe, Asia, or America. Approximately half of the world population speaks languages which derive from the Indo-European language family. The second largest language family is the Sino-Tibetan family, which primarily encompasses languages which developed in Eastern Asia. The Sino-Tibetan language family includes languages spoken by a quarter of the world population. The remaining language families are Niger-Congo languages (developed in Sub-Saharan Africa), Afro-Asiatic languages (developed in North Africa and into Southwest Asia), Austronesian languages (developed in Australia and surrounding islands), Dravidian languages (developed in South Asia), Austro-Asiatic languages (developed in Southeast Asia), and Japonic languages (developed in Japan).

In contrast, regional languages are languages that are spoken in a specific region. Essentially, regional languages are spoken by a subset of the larger population. They are localized to a certain geographic area.

Although regional languages are spoken by a subset of a population, this does not necessarily mean that they are spoken by few people. For example, Wu, a regional language spoken in a Chinese province, is spoken by more than 90 million people. By comparison, this means that it is spoken by more people than speak French. Another example of a regional language is Welsh.

 *Sample Test Questions*

1) The Ring of Fire describes a band of volcanoes that surround the

    A) Atlantic Ocean
    B) Indian Ocean
    C) Mediterranean Ocean
    D) Pacific Ocean

The correct answer is D:) Pacific Ocean. The Ring of Fire circumscribes the Pacific Ocean. There is also a string of volcanoes around the Mediterranean Ocean, but it is not called the Ring of Fire.

2) The principal means of transporting sediments is

    A) Wind
    B) Water
    C) Gravity
    D) Storms

The correct answer is B:) Water. Water – in streams and glaciers, underground, and in ocean currents – is the principal means of transporting material from one place to another.

3) Which of the following is NOT a result of glaciers?

    A) Moraines
    B) V-shaped valleys
    C) Striations
    D) All of the above are results of glaciers

The correct answer is B:) V-shaped valleys. Glaciers result in U-shaped valleys; rivers result in V-shaped valleys.

4) What climate is most conducive to chemical weathering?

    A) Cold, wet climates
    B) Cold, arid climates
    C) Hot, wet climates
    D) Hot, dry climates

The correct answer is C:) Hot, wet climates. The heat acts as a type of catalyst in speeding the chemical reactions which break down the minerals, many of which require water.

5) As altitude increases, climatic conditions become

    A) Drier and colder
    B) Drier and warmer
    C) Wetter and colder
    D) Wetter and warmer

The correct answer is A:) Drier and colder. As altitude increases, climatic conditions become increasingly drier and colder.

6) A general characteristic of river development is

    A) Valleys tend to be deeper and narrower at the headwaters of a river
    B) Sediment load is greatest at the headwaters and decreases downstream
    C) Steep slopes lead to the development of meandering streams
    D) Wider valleys are cut at the headwaters and narrower ones downstream

The correct answer is A:) Valleys tend to be deeper and narrower at the headwaters of a river. The headwaters of a river tend to have deeper, narrower valleys that you find downstream.

7) A rich habitat at the mouth of a river is called a(n)

    A) Swamp
    B) Marsh
    C) Estuary
    D) Fjord

The correct answer is C:) Estuary. A highly productive marshy habitat near the mouth of a river is called an estuary.

8) An aquifer is

   A) The same as groundwater
   B) The upper surface of the zone saturated with groundwater
   C) A permeable rock formation trapped between rock layers that are impermeable
   D) The force of gravity moving water through the layers of rock and soil

The correct answer is C:) A permeable rock formation trapped between rock layers that are impermeable. An aquifer is a layer of permeable rock trapped between two layers of impermeable rock. Groundwater fills the pore spaces in the permeable rock.

9) Which statement best explains why Eugene, Oregon and Trenton, New Jersey, two cities with nearly the same latitude, have different climates?

   A) They are at different longitudes
   B) They are near different ocean currents
   C) They have different elevations
   D) They have different numbers of daylight hours

The correct answer is B:) They are near different ocean currents. Eugene is at a latitude of 44 while Trenton is at a latitude of 40, so their latitudes are very close. Their difference in elevation of 350 feet does not account for their differences in climate nearly as much as the difference between the Gulf Stream and the California Current.

10) Non-living renewable resources include

   A) Metals, oil, and water
   B) Minerals, air, and water
   C) Soil, air, and water
   D) Salt, coal, and iron

The correct answer is C:) Soil, air and water. Non-living renewable resources include water, air, and soil.

11) Geography is directly concerned with

    A) Location
    B) Time frame
    C) Motivation
    D) None of the above

The correct answer is A:) Location. What it all comes down to is that geography attempts to explain human actions as they are caused by, relate to, and affect one thing – location.

12) The most common belief system in the United States BESIDES Christianity is

    A) Buddhism
    B) Judaism
    C) Islam
    D) None of the above

The correct answer is D:) None of the above. The second largest group in the United States is the non-religious sector, which comprises between 10 and 15 percent of the population.

13) Gerrymandering is an attempt to influence

    A) Voting
    B) Law making
    C) School standards
    D) Prison conditions

The correct answer is A:) Voting. Gerrymandering is an attempt to establish a political advantage for a particular candidate or individual by drawing voting districts to be most advantageous.

14) Which of the following is an example of the uses of geography in the world today?

    A) Neoclassicism
    B) Gerrymandering
    C) Revolutionism
    D) None of the above

The correct answer is B:) Gerrymandering. Gerrymandering is an attempt to establish a political advantage for a particular candidate or individual by drawing voting districts to be most advantageous.

15) Which of the following was NOT a plant domesticated in Mesoamerica?

    A) Squash
    B) Corn
    C) Beans
    D) Sunflower

The correct answer is D:) Sunflower. The sunflower was domesticated in the eastern part of North America, not in Mesoamerica.

16) Which of the following sets most correctly identifies crops domesticated in North America?

    A) Chocolate, cotton, sugar, maize
    B) Maize, marshelder, squash, sunflower
    C) Sunflower, potatoes, indigo, rice
    D) Tobacco, sugar, potatoes, maize

The correct answer is B:) Maize, marshelder, squash, sunflower. Domestication of crops in North America occurred both in the east (e.g., sunflower, marshelder, chenopod, etc.), and moving up from Mesoamerica (e.g., maize and beans).

17) Which of the following would NOT be a typical crop of Mediterranean agriculture?

   A) Barley
   B) Grapes
   C) Potatoes
   D) Figs

The correct answer is C:) Potatoes. Barley, grapes, and figs are all important staples of Mediterranean agriculture.

18) According to Clark's model, transitional countries are characterized by a focus on activities in which sector?

   A) Primary
   B) Secondary
   C) Tertiary
   D) Quaternary

The correct answer is B:) Secondary. The secondary sector is the manufacturing and construction sector.

19) What was the approximate world population in 10,000 BC?

   A) No estimates exist
   B) 1 million
   C) 10 million
   D) 100 million

The correct answer is C:) 10 million. This is only about 1.5 percent of the current world population.

20) Approximately when are the first humans dated to?

   A) 10-20 million years ago
   B) 50-100 million years ago
   C) 150-200 million years ago
   D) 500 million years ago

The correct answer is C:) 150-200 million years ago.

21) Which of the following is studied in relation to geography?

 A) Nature
 B) Space
 C) Population
 D) All of the above

The correct answer is D:) All of the above. Geography considers a multitude of factors in the extent that they relate to human populations.

22) Where is the "cradle of the human race"?

 A) Asia
 B) Mesoamerica
 C) Mesopotamia
 D) Africa

The correct answer is D:) Africa. From here, human populations spread first to Asia, and later to Europe and the Americas.

23) The classification of primate city is given to cities which are how much larger than the next largest city in a nation?

 A) 1.5 times
 B) 2 times
 C) 4 times
 D) 6 times

The correct answer is B:) 2 times. Of course, many primate cities today are as much as seven times larger than their nearest competitors.

24) Which of the following is NOT considered a primate city?

 A) London
 B) Mexico City
 C) Paris
 D) Los Angeles

The correct answer is D:) Los Angeles. New York is larger than Los Angeles so it cannot be a primate city.

25) Which of the following is NOT one of the five urban hearths?

    A) Fertile Crescent
    B) Mesoamerica
    C) Scandinavia
    D) Indus River Valley

The correct answer is C:) Scandinavia. The urban hearths are the Fertile Crescent, Nile River Valley, Indus River Valley, China, and Mesoamerica.

26) Where did Confucianism originate?

    A) China
    B) India
    C) Tibet
    D) Japan

The correct answer is A:) China. Confucianism originated in approximately the 5th century BC in China.

27) Which of the following is NOT true of Buddhism?

    A) It is based on the teachings of Siddhartha Gautama, who came to be known as Buddha.
    B) It focuses mainly on strengthening the bonds of familial ties, and loyalty to friends and family.
    C) It emphasizes that life is suffering, and pleasure is only temporary.
    D) It has the goal of achieving a state of detachment known as Nirvana.

The correct answer is B:) It focuses mainly on strengthening bonds of familial ties, and loyalty to friends and family. This is more correctly descriptive of Confucianism than Buddhism.

28) Which of the following best describes population distribution in 10,000 BC?

    A) Human populations were localized to Sub-Saharan Africa.
    B) Human populations were beginning to spread into Europe from Sub-Saharan Africa.
    C) Human populations were in various parts of the earth.
    D) Human populations are not documented until 5,000 BC.

The correct answer is C:) Human populations were in various parts of the earth. However, they existed in significantly smaller numbers than today.

29) Which of the following is NOT a universal religion?

    A) Islam
    B) Catholicism
    C) Protestantism
    D) Judaism

The correct answer is D:) Judaism. Universal religions have a goal of converting as many people as possible, which is not the case with Judaism.

30) Which of the following BEST describes universal religions?

    A) Self-contained
    B) Conversion-oriented
    C) Has multiple deities
    D) Often changing

The correct answer is B:) Conversion-oriented. Religions which are aimed at preaching their message and converting as many people as possible are universal religions.

31) What is the primary religion of India?

    A) Buddhism
    B) Muslim
    C) Hinduism
    D) Confucianism

The correct answer is C:) Hinduism. Approximately 80 percent of the population is Hindu.

32) What is the second largest religion in India?

    A) Buddhism
    B) Muslim
    C) Hinduism
    D) Confucianism

The correct answer is B:) Muslim. Approximately 13 percent of the population is Muslim.

33) According to Thomas Malthus

    A) Human populations evolved in Asian rather than in African regions.
    B) Populations are naturally limited based on the availability of resources.
    C) Cities evolve with a central business district in the center, surrounded by other zones.
    D) Dependency ratios describe the inherent limitations of a population.

The correct answer is B:) Populations are naturally limited based on the availability of resources. He theorized that because the world's resources increase at a constant, or linear, rate and the world's population grows exponentially, that there will come a point when there will not be enough resources to support the world's growing population.

34) Approximately what percent of individuals in the United States identify themselves as Christian?

    A) 80 percent
    B) 66 percent
    C) 50 percent
    D) 40 percent

The correct answer is A:) 80 percent. Christianity is by a wide margin the most widely held belief system in the United States.

35) If a nation has a population of 5 million, 2.3 million of which are dependents, what is the dependency ratio?

    A) .14
    B) .07
    C) 1.17
    D) .85

The correct answer is D:) .85. The dependency ratio is the number of dependents (2.3 million) divided by the number of non-dependents (in this case 2.7 million) in a population.

36) World Systems Theory was developed by

    A) Wallerstein
    B) Rostow
    C) Clarke
    D) Friedman

The correct answer is A:) Wallerstein.

37) Which of the following is NOT true of Confucianism?

    A) It is associated with a series of kind-hearted deities.
    B) It had an important influence in shaping social behaviors and norms in China.
    C) Confucius himself spent his life traveling with a small group of followers and teaching the children of dignitaries.
    D) Confucianism is conservative and emphasizes the importance of respect and loyalty in relationships.

The correct answer is A:) It is associated with a series of kind-hearted deities. Confucianism is not associated with any deities.

38) According to Wallerstein, the exploitation of peripheral areas characterizes the

    A) First stage of development
    B) Second stage of development
    C) Third and fourth stages of development
    D) Fifth stage of development

The correct answer is C:) Third and fourth stages of development. There is no fifth stage, and exploitation doesn't begin until the third and fourth stages.

39) Which stage of Rostow's developmental model is characterized by the beginnings of industrialization and a small amount of mobility?

    A) Traditional Society
    B) Transitional Stage
    C) Take Off
    D) Drive to Maturity

The correct answer is B:) Transitional Stage. This stage is also referred to as the Preconditions for Take-Off stage and is the second stage of Rostow's model.

40) Today's developed, core regions are in which stage of Rostow's model?

    A) Take-Off
    B) Traditional Society
    C) Age of Mass Consumption
    D) Drive to Maturity

The correct answer is C:) Age of Mass Consumption. This is the fifth and final stage of Rostow's model. It is characterized by a strong service sector of the economy.

41) Where did Buddhism originate?

    A) China
    B) India
    C) Tibet
    D) Japan

The correct answer is B:) India. The origins of Buddhism can be traced back to the 5th century BC in India. It is based on the teachings of a man named Siddhartha Gautama, who came to be known as Buddha.

42) Education and health care are a part of the

    A) Primary sector
    B) Secondary sector
    C) Tertiary sector
    D) Quaternary sector

The correct answer is C:) Tertiary sector. The tertiary sector is the service sector, which includes both education and health care.

43) John Friedman developed a Model of Regional Development which categorized regions into what four stages?

    A) Pre-industrial, transitional, industrial, and post-industrial
    B) Pre-industrial, core, periphery, and semi-periphery
    C) Proto-industrial, industrializing, transitional, and core
    D) Post-industrial, periphery, transitional, and core

The correct answer is A:) Pre-industrial, transitional, industrial, and post-industrial.

44) Which of the following describes Stage 3 of Friedman's Model of Regional Development

    A) Low economic and social mobility
    B) Hunter/gatherer techniques and agricultural focus
    C) Development of multiple cores which trade with the original core settlement
    D) A specialized, functioning, fully integrated economy

The correct answer is C:) Development of multiple cores which trade with the original core settlement. Answers A and B describe Stage 1, and answer D describes Stage 4.

45) Which of the following is NOT considered to be a part of the core?

    A) United States
    B) Britain
    C) Russia
    D) Canada

The correct answer is C:) Russia. The core consists of Europe, the United States, Canada, Australia, Japan, Israel, and a few others.

46) Mexico is considered to be a part of the

    A) Periphery
    B) Semi-periphery
    C) Core
    D) None of the above

The correct answer is A:) Periphery.

47) Christaller's Central Place Theory uses a _____ model to describe the relationship of central places.

    A) Circular
    B) Square
    C) Triangular
    D) Hexagonal

The correct answer is D:) Hexagonal. Any other shape would leave gaps where people had no access to a central place.

48) The maximum distance that people are willing to travel to obtain a good or service is referred to as what?

    A) Hinterland
    B) Range
    C) Threshold
    D) Gravitation distance

The correct answer is B:) Range. The threshold is the distance that a business needs them to travel to sustain their activities.

49) The sector model of urban development is characterized by

    A) Sectors of concentric zones
    B) Wedges branching out in sectors
    C) Hexagonal groupings of sectors
    D) None of the above

The correct answer is B:) Wedges branching out in sectors. This sector model was developed by Hoyt.

50) The highest priced land in the sector model is found in which sector?

    A) CBD
    B) Industrial
    C) Middle class residential
    D) High class residential

The correct answer is A:) CBD. This is because of its central location and the presence of commercial areas.

51) The Burgess model of urban development is characterized by

    A) Concentric zones
    B) Wedges branching out in sectors
    C) Hexagonal groupings
    D) None of the above

The correct answer is A:) Concentric zones. The Burgess model is also known as the concentric zone model.

52) What surrounds the central business district according to the concentric zone model?

    A) Working class housing
    B) Low income housing
    C) The industrial sector
    D) Suburban housing

The correct answer is C:) The industrial sector. This is then followed by various stages of housing.

53) The area with the lowest population density in North American cities is

    A) At the center of the urban area
    B) A ring around the CBD
    C) A wedge moving out from the CBD
    D) On the outskirts

The correct answer is A:) At the center of the urban area. This is the CBD and is occupied by business rather than people.

54) Which of the following would be a push factor?

    A) Drought
    B) Famine
    C) War
    D) All of the above

The correct answer is D:) All of the above. Drought, famine, and war are all factors that would motivate an individual to leave an area. This makes them all push factors.

55) Which of the following sets of crops is most characteristic of Mediterranean agriculture?

    A) Citrus, barley, figs, olives, and grapes
    B) Cocoa, maize, sugar, and squash
    C) Maize, sunflower, tobacco, olives, and rice
    D) Potatoes, cocoa, cotton, and figs

The correct answer is A:) Citrus, barley, figs, olives, and grapes. Also important in Mediterranean agriculture are wheat, and dates.

56) Which of the following is a non-renewable resource?

    A) Solar power
    B) Metals
    C) Natural gas
    D) Tidal waves

The correct answer is C:) Natural gas. Fossil fuels (natural gas, petroleum, and coal) are all examples of non-renewable resources.

57) Which of the following statements is FALSE?

    A) Because trees can be replanted, they are a renewable resource.
    B) Non-renewable resources such as coal cannot be used sustainably at current demand.
    C) Because specific rays of sunlight can only be used once it is considered a non-renewable resource.
    D) None of the above

The correct answer is C:) Because specific rays of sunlight can only be used once it is considered a non-renewable resource. Sunlight is a renewable resource, as are tidal waves, wind, metal, and timber.

58) How are mongoose populations regarded in African countries?

    A) They are a dangerous pest which destroy crops and harm populations.
    B) They are a popular pet because they are so docile.
    C) They are protective because they are known for fighting and eating venomous snakes.
    D) None of the above

The correct answer is C:) They are protective because they are known for fighting and eating venomous snakes. They diet also includes the occasional crocodile egg and carrion.

59) Temperate zones are characterized by

    A) Consistent, direct sunlight
    B) Inconsistent, direct sunlight
    C) Consistent, indirect sunlight
    D) Inconsistent, indirect sunlight

The correct answer is C:) Consistent, indirect sunlight. Although temperate areas do not receive direct sunlight, they do receive a fair and consistent amount of sunlight each day.

60) Which of the following cities is located between 40-60 degrees north/south latitude and is warm in July and cool in January?

A) New York
B) Buenos Aires
C) Zimbabwe
D) New Deli

The correct answer is A:) New York. The area described is the Northern Temperate Zone.

61) Which of the following countries would have four seasons in a year, with the cold season around July?

A) Ecuador
B) Canada
C) Norway
D) Argentina

The correct answer is D:) Argentina. This describes the Southern Temperate Zone.

62) Which of the following countries has a climate characterized by consistent sunlight and warm or mild, year-round temperatures?

A) India
B) Greenland
C) Sweden
D) Australia

The correct answer is A:) India. This describes the tropical climate zones (near the equator).

63) When a contour line comes to a "V" directed downhill this indicates a

A) Ridge
B) River
C) Gulley
D) Valley

The correct answer is A:) Ridge. Contour lines are used to show differences in elevation.

64) When a contour line comes to a "V" directed uphill this indicates a

A) Ridge
B) River
C) Gulley
D) Valley

The correct answer is D:) Valley. Contour lines are used to show differences in elevation.

65) Which of the following diseases is associated with tropical climates?

A) Yellow fever
B) HIV
C) Polio
D) All of the above

The correct answer is A:) Yellow fever. Other tropical diseases include malaria, dengue fever, and cholera.

66) Which of the following countries is resource-rich and developing?

A) China
B) Russia
C) Venezuela
D) Britain

The correct answer is C:) Venezuela. Although Venezuela is very resource-rich, the distribution of wealth leaves much of the country in poverty.

67) Which of the following countries has a limited water supply?

A) Bahrain
B) Iceland
C) Switzerland
D) Holland

The correct answer is A:) Bahrain. Other countries with little access to water include Kenya, Saudi Arabia, Kuwait, Algeria, and Libya.

68) Burkina Faso was originally a colony of

    A) Austria
    B) Britain
    C) Germany
    D) France

The correct answer is D:) France. Burkina Faso declared independence in 1960.

69) Burkina Faso is located on which continent?

    A) Europe
    B) Africa
    C) Asia
    D) South America

The correct answer is B:) Africa. Burkina Faso bordered to the south by Ghana and to the east by Niger.

70) Which of the following is a correct comparison to the size of Russia?

    A) Four times the United States
    B) Half the size of China
    C) Triple the size of Germany
    D) Half the size of Africa

The correct answer is D:) Half the size of Africa. Russia is double the size of the US or China, and is half the size of the African continent.

71) Which of the following could NOT be said of Russia?

    A) It is night in all of Russia for an average of 1 hour each evening.
    B) The land area of Russia is about 17 million kilometers.
    C) Russia is double size of the United States.
    D) All of the above are true.

The correct answer is A:) It is night in all of Russia for an average of 1 hour each evening. The sun technically never sets over all of Russia at once.

72) How many South American countries are landlocked?

    A) 0
    B) 2
    C) 3
    D) 4

The correct answer is B:) 2.

73) Which of the following South American countries is landlocked?

    A) Bolivia
    B) Argentina
    C) Ecuador
    D) Venezuela

The correct answer is A:) Bolivia. Paraguay is also landlocked.

74) Which of the following is FALSE?

    A) The Prime Meridian is 0 degrees longitude
    B) Longitude lines describe location north or south of the equator
    C) Latitude lines run from 0 to 90 degrees north and south
    D) Longitude lines run from 0 to 90 degrees east and west

The correct answer is D:) Longitude lines run from 0 to 90 degrees east and west. Longitude lines range from 0 to 180 degrees.

75) Which of the following map lines are also referred to as parallels?

    A) Contour lines
    B) Meridians
    C) Longitude
    D) Latitude

The correct answer is D:) Latitude. Lines of latitude, or parallels, run from north to south on a map.

76) Lines on a map which outline areas of equal temperature are called

    A) Isotherm lines
    B) Isobar lines
    C) Cut-contour lines
    D) Latitude

The correct answer is A:) Isotherm lines. Isotherm originates from "iso" for same and "therm" for temperature.

77) A map which outlines a region based on isothermal properties would be based on

    A) Wind patterns
    B) Snowfall
    C) Temperatures
    D) Population

The correct answer is C:) Temperatures. Isotherm originates from "iso" for same and "therm" for temperature.

78) Which type of display represents the surface of the Earth most accurately?

    A) Flat map
    B) Globe
    C) Longitudinal map
    D) None of the above

The correct answer is B:) Globe. Globes are the most accurate because they can show the actual shape of landmasses. However, they have far less detail than other forms of maps.

79) Which of the following is NOT an advantage of a flat map over a globe?

    A) Easier to use in judging distances
    B) More portable than globes
    C) More accurate representation of space
    D) None of the above

The correct answer is C:) More accurate representation of space. Globes represent space more accurately than flat maps.

80) The urban hierarchy ranks cities into four different sizes with the most central and urban areas being termed

A) First order
B) Second order
C) Third order
D) Fourth order

The correct answer is D:) Fourth order.

81) Second order urban centers in the urban hierarchy are also referred to as

A) Hamlets
B) Villages
C) Towns
D) Cities

The correct answer is B:) Villages. The influence of a second order center may extend to a number of first order centers which will travel to them for services.

82) The uncontrolled and unplanned outward spreading of a city is

A) Urban sprawl
B) Urban hierarchy
C) Concentric zones urban model
D) Urban heat island

The correct answer is A:) Urban sprawl. Urban sprawl is typically looked on with a negative connotation.

83) Urban sprawl is what type of diffusion?

A) Relocation diffusion
B) Hierarchical diffusion
C) Stimulus diffusion
D) Spatial diffusion

The correct answer is D:) Spatial diffusion.

84) If a song becomes popular in a number of major cities across the world around the same time as a result of being placed on the internet it would be an example of

    A) Hierarchical diffusion
    B) Stimulus diffusion
    C) Contagious diffusion
    D) Relocation diffusion

The correct answer is C:) Contagious diffusion. Contagious diffusion is a rapid, widespread diffusion of a characteristic throughout a population.

85) Which of the following is NOT one of the types of diffusion?

    A) Hierarchical diffusion
    B) Stimulus diffusion
    C) Voidal diffusion
    D) Relocation diffusion

The correct answer is C:) Voidal diffusion. The major types of diffusion are relocation diffusion, expansion diffusion, stimulus diffusion, hierarchical diffusion, and contagious diffusion.

86) Which of the following is NOT a contributing factor to urban heat islands?

    A) The removal of vegetation in heavily urbanized areas.
    B) Feedback from buildings and roads.
    C) Increased production of greenhouse gases.
    D) All of the above contribute to the urban heat island phenomenon.

The correct answer is D:) All of the above contribute to the urban heat island phenomenon.

87) Which of the following best describes an urban heat island?

    A) Islands with highly urbanized populations such as Japan and Hawaii.
    B) A "hot spot" on the surface of the earth that is caused by urbanization.
    C) The central city of a nation creates an "island" of urbanization.
    D) None of the above

The correct answer is B:) A "hot spot" on the surface of the earth that is caused by urbanization. Urban heat islands have hotter temperatures than less urbanized surrounding areas.

88) A country with a high HDI and a stable economy is

    A) Underdeveloped
    B) Developing
    C) LDC
    D) Developed

The correct answer is D:) Developed. HDI is the Human Development Index.

89) Which of the following is most likely NOT classified as an LDC?

    A) Cambodia
    B) Laos
    C) Germany
    D) Cambodia

The correct answer is C:) Germany. LDC stands for Less Developed Country.

90) Which of the following is NOT a major megalopolis area of the United States?

    A) Boston-New York-Washington
    B) Atlanta-Huston-Raleigh
    C) Fresno-Sacramento-San Francisco
    D) Chicago-Detroit-Pittsburgh

The correct answer is B:) Atlanta-Huston-Raleigh. The largest megalopolis in the United States is "BosNyWash," comprised of the Boston-New York-Washing area.

91) Which of the following was never a colony of a European nation?

    A) South Africa
    B) Azerbaijan
    C) Congo
    D) Virgin Islands

The correct answer is B:) Azerbaijan. South Africa, Congo, and the Virgin Islands have been (or in the case of the Virgin Islands, still are) are colonies of a European nation.

92) When a country directly settles and populates an area, so that the area becomes an extension of the mother country, this is

    A) Subjectivism
    B) Imperialism
    C) Monarchism
    D) Colonialism

The correct answer is D:) Colonialism. Imperialism is when one country takes control of another country that it is not adjacent to.

93) Which of the following country shapes is the most efficient?

    A) Large and spread out, like the United States
    B) Long and thin, like Chile
    C) Small and compact, like Greece
    D) None of the above

The correct answer is C:) Small and compact, like Greece. This allows the government to easily maintain control and keep the populations interests in unison.

94) Which of the following is NOT a problem that develops as a country grows large?

    A) Technological difficulty of communication
    B) Logistical difficulty for governments to maintain power
    C) The development of regional interests
    D) All of the above problems arise

The correct answer is D:) All of the above problems arise. This is why the most efficient country shape is small, compact, and roughly round.

95) Which of the following are NOT associated with high elevation?

    A) Plateau
    B) Mountain
    C) Plain
    D) Neither A nor C

The correct answer is C:) Plain. Plateaus and mountains are both associated with high elevations. However, valleys and plains are associated with lower elevations.

96) Erosion is

    A) The movement of sediments
    B) The breaking down of large rock formations
    C) The decomposition of rocks into soils and minerals
    D) None of the above

The correct answer is A:) The movement of sediments. Erosion should not be confused with weathering.

97) As water heats and condenses to water vapor, which type of severe storm is fueled?

    A) Hurricane
    B) Monsoon
    C) Thunder storm
    D) Tornado

The correct answer is A:) Hurricane. Hurricanes can be compared to a tornado which develops over water.

98) The most noticeable and visible evidence of the motion of plate tectonics is located where?

    A) Sub-Saharan Africa
    B) Pacific Ocean
    C) Atlantic Ocean
    D) Southeast Asia

The correct answer is B:) Pacific Ocean. More specifically, the Ring of Fire.

99) Where is the Ring of Fire located?

    A) Pacific Ocean
    B) Gobi Desert
    C) Chile's Atacama Desert
    D) Mediterranean Sea

The correct answer is A:) Pacific Ocean. The Ring of Fire is a large circle of volcanoes formed along the edge of the Pacific plate.

100) A seasonal change in winds perpetuates and exacerbates the rainy season in Southeast Asia, resulting in which type of severe weather phenomenon?

    A) Thunder storms
    B) Cyclone
    C) Typhoon
    D) Monsoon

The correct answer is D:) Monsoon. Monsoons flood rivers and other bodies of water which can wipe out entire communities.

101) Thunder storms are caused as

    A) Cold air rises
    B) Hot and cold air collide
    C) Hot air rises
    D) Static clouds meet a cold, rain front

The correct answer is C:) Hot air rises. For this reason, thunder storms typically occur in the early evening.

102) Which state is most likely to have a tornado?

    A) Oklahoma
    B) California
    C) Florida
    D) Maine

The correct answer is A:) Oklahoma. Tornadoes are most common in the central United States in an area known as Tornado Alley.

103) Which state is most likely to have a thunderstorm?

    A) Oklahoma
    B) California
    C) Florida
    D) Maine

The correct answer is C:) Florida. Florida is known for thunderstorms because cool ocean breezes push in from both directions, creating ideal conditions for them.

104) Which state is most likely to have an earthquake?

    A) Oklahoma
    B) California
    C) Florida
    D) Maine

The correct answer is B:) California. The famous San Andreas Fault runs through California.

105) Continental weather is _____ and _____ than maritime weather.

    A) Less stable/less mild
    B) Less stable/more mild
    C) More stable/less mild
    D) More stable/more mild

The correct answer is A:) Less stable/less mild. The temperatures in continental areas tends to vary more between day and night, getting hotter and cooler than in maritime areas.

106) The fact that continental areas tend to get warmer because the land absorbs heat and therefore heats the air is referred to as

    A) Negative feedback
    B) Positive feedback
    C) Heat feedback
    D) Urban feedback

The correct answer is B:) Positive feedback. For this reason, maritime areas have a milder climate.

107) Soil which arid and dry is known as

    A) Desert
    B) Aridisol
    C) Sand
    D) Artesia

The correct answer is B:) Aridisol. The term aridisol is used in United States soil classification.

108) Aridisols would NOT be found in which state?

   A) Nevada
   B) Wyoming
   C) Oklahoma
   D) New Mexico

The correct answer is C:) Oklahoma. Aridisols are found primarily in the western part of the United States, in the states of Arizona, Utah, New Mexico, Nevada, Colorado and Wyoming.

109) The largest biome is the

   A) Savanna
   B) Taiga
   C) Tropical Rainforest
   D) Chaparral

The correct answer is B:) Taiga. The Taiga spans much of Russia and Canada and is characterized by cold evergreen forests.

110) Tall trees which don't branch until at least 100 feet up, and which support a stunning diversity of wildlife are found in

   A) Alpine
   B) Savanna
   C) Tropical Rainforest
   D) Tundra

The correct answer is C:) Tropical Rainforest. Trees in the tropical rainforest can be up to 250 feet, with smaller shrubs beneath where there are breaks in the canopy of trees.

111) Which biome is primarily found near the Tropics of Cancer and Capricorn?

   A) Savanna
   B) Desert
   C) Tundra
   D) Alpine

The correct answer is B:) Desert. This location allows for the consistent direct sunlight of the equator with the colder, windier characteristics of the temperate zones.

112) The most common material with which caves are formed is

A) Lava
B) Metamorphic rock
C) Ice
D) Limestone

The correct answer is D:) Limestone. Limestone caves are not only the most common, but also the largest and longest types of caves.

113) Which of the following is NOT one of the main types of caves?

A) Lithographic caves
B) Sea caves
C) Ice caves
D) Lava caves

The correct answer is A:) Lithographic caves. The four main types of caves are limestone caves, lava caves, sea caves, and ice caves.

114) Which of the following is NOT an example of a rain shadow?

A) The Gobi Desert
B) Death Valley, California
C) Atacama Desert
D) All of the above are examples of rain shadow

The correct answer is D:) All of the above are examples of rain shadow. Rain shadows are created when mountains create a barrier for storms moving over an area.

115) Communities located in a rain shadow would most likely

A) Be wasteful of water due to its abundance.
B) Use and collect water efficiently.
C) Spend the majority of their day preparing heavy, water-resistant clothing.
D) All of the above

The correct answer is B:) Use and collect water efficiently. Rain shadows are desert areas. This would force communities to be highly conscious of water usage.

116) Population growth of greater than 2-3 percent would not be expected in

A) Nigeria
B) South Africa
C) Russia
D) Kenya

The correct answer is C:) Russia. Russia and other areas of Europe have even been known to have negative population growth rates. High growth rates such as 3 percent are more typical of Africa.

117) The areas of Western Europe, North America, and China have a typical population growth rate of

A) Greater than 5 percent
B) 2-3 percent
C) Less than 1 percent
D) The three have very different typical population growth rates

The correct answer is C:) Less than 1 percent. Growth rates of 2-3 percent are typical in Africa, and rates of 1-2 percent are typical in South America, Australia, and the Middle East.

118) Which of the following would NOT be considered a refugee?

A) An individual who leaves their country because a war starts and they are in danger.
B) An individual who leaves their country because they get a better job offer elsewhere.
C) An individual who leaves their country following a large tsunami that destroys their home.
D) An individual who leaves their country because of intense persecution.

The correct answer is B:) An individual who leaves their country because they get a better job offer elsewhere. This person would more correctly be considered an emigrant than a refugee.

119) An individual who is forced to leave their home is a

    A) Emigrant
    B) Migrant
    C) Immigrant
    D) Refugee

The correct answer is D:) Refugee. Refugees may be forced to leave their homes by war, persecution, natural disasters, or other factors.

120) Doubling time refers to

    A) The number of years before a population will double in size.
    B) The number of years it will take for a city to double in population.
    C) The number of years until a city doubles in terms of geographic area.
    D) The number of years that it has taken for a population to double in size.

The correct answer is A:) The number of years before a population will double in size. For example, the doubling time of a population will a growth rate of 1 percent will double in approximately 70 years.

121) A population with a growth rate of 5 percent would have a doubling time of

    A) 35
    B) 20
    C) 14
    D) 5

The correct answer is C:) 14. Doubling time can be approximated by the equation $n=70/r$.

122) Which biome is most similar to a taiga?

    A) Alpines
    B) Tropical Rainforest
    C) Savannas
    D) Tundras

The correct answer is A:) Alpines. Alpines are essentially a taiga except in the mountains instead of the Arctics.

123) In which of the following countries is the mongoose an important element both to human populations and culture?

A) Egypt
B) United States
C) Argentina
D) Britain

The correct answer is A:) Egypt. The mongoose is found in Africa and areas of the Middle East.

124) Push and pull factors are related to

A) Climate change
B) The spread of disease
C) Immigration
D) Ocean tides

The correct answer is C:) Immigration. Push and pull factors are things that motivate a person to move to a different area.

125) An epidemic can be described as something that

A) Is found in a specific geographic region
B) Is a consistently recurring problem
C) Causes widespread panic and confusion
D) Spreads over a large space relatively quickly

The correct answer is D:) Spreads over a large space relatively quickly. Answers A and B better describe the term endemic, and answer C describes pandemic.

126) The most widely used language family is the

A) Indo-European
B) Sino-Tibetan
C) Indo-Asiatic
D) Afro-Asiatic

The correct answer is A:) Indo-European. Approximately half of the world's population speaks languages traced to the Indo-European language family.

127) Which of the following is a regional language?

    A) French
    B) Welsh
    C) Austronesian languages
    D) All of the above

The correct answer is B:) Welsh. French is the national language of France and Austronesian languages are a language family. Welsh, on the other hand, is a regional language of Wales.

128) Which continent does NOT have a cultural hearth?

    A) Australia
    B) Asia
    C) Africa
    D) South America

The correct answer is A:) Australia.

129) Which of the following is NOT one of the seven ancient cultural hearths?

    A) Mesopotamia
    B) Andean America
    C) Mesoamerica
    D) Northeastern Europe

The correct answer is D:) Northeastern Europe. The seven hearths are the Nile Valley or Indus Valley, Wei-Huang Valley, Ganges Valley, Mesopotamia, Mesoamerica, West Africa, and Andean America.

130) The ozone shields the earth from

    A) CFCs
    B) UV rays
    C) Interspace particles
    D) Gamma rays

The correct answer is B:) UV Rays.

131) Chlorofluorocarbons (CFC's) deplete the

    A) Ozone layer
    B) Lithosphere
    C) Stratosphere
    D) Methosphere

The correct answer is A:) Ozone layer. The ozone layer is essential in protecting the earth from harmful UV rays, and it is depleted by CFC's.

132) OPEC regulates the price and availability of

    A) Diamonds
    B) Coal
    C) Oil
    D) Wheat

The correct answer is C:) Oil. OPEC is essentially an international cartel of oil-exporting countries which works to manipulate the price and availability of oil to the best benefit of members.

133) Which of the following countries is NOT a member of OPEC?

    A) Saudi Arabia
    B) Egypt
    C) Venezuela
    D) Iraq

The correct answer is B:) Egypt. The five founding countries of OPEC are Iran, Iraq, Kuwait, Saudi Arabia, and Venezuela.

134) How many species are considered to be domesticated?

    A) 10
    B) 30
    C) 100
    D) 200

The correct answer is B:) 30. Fewer than 30 species have been domesticated, including dogs, sheep, cattle, goats, chickens, donkeys, bees, camels, and horses.

135) Which of the following is NOT a domesticated animal?

    A) Wolf
    B) Camel
    C) Llama
    D) Bee

The correct answer is A:) Wolf. Other domesticated animals include dogs, cats, sheep, goats, and horses.

136) Which of the following is NOT a type of economic system?

    A) Subsistence
    B) Culture
    C) Market
    D) Planned

The correct answer is B:) Culture. The four economic systems are subsistence (traditional), commercial (market or capitalist), planned (centrally planned or socialist), and mixed.

137) The United States is most correctly classified as which type of economic system?

    A) Subsistence
    B) Capitalist
    C) Planned
    D) Mixed

The correct answer is D:) Mixed. Mixed systems are mostly capitalist systems that allow for government intervention, as in the United States with taxes, etc.

138) Tropical diseases are often spread by

    A) Human touch
    B) Insects and parasites
    C) Sexual contact
    D) Waste

The correct answer is B:) Insects and parasites. For example, malaria is spread by mosquitoes.

139) Which of the following correctly identifies a benefit of moving nuclear plants to rural, rather than urban areas?

    A) More effective use of land
    B) Avoids falling property values in cities
    C) Safer
    D) All of the above

The correct answer is D:) All of the above. Each of the answers describes a benefit of moving nuclear plants to rural areas.

140) Fear of the waste produced is a complaint against

    A) Centrifugal forces
    B) Maritime patterns
    C) Demographic transition
    D) Nuclear plants

The correct answer is D:) Nuclear plants.

141) Reciting the Pledge of Allegiance in schools is an example of a

    A) Disseminative force
    B) Centripetal force
    C) Urbanizing force
    D) Centrifugal force

The correct answer is B:) Centripetal force. Centripetal forces, such as a feeling of nationalism and loyalty to country, unify a nation.

142) The Atacama Desert is an example of a

    A) Polar desert
    B) Trade wind desert
    C) West coast desert
    D) Rainshadow desert

The correct answer is C:) West coast desert. The Atacama Desert is the driest place on earth, receiving as little as 1 mm of rain every 5-20 years.

143) West coast deserts are primarily found

   A) Along the Equator
   B) Near the Tropics of Cancer and Capricorn
   C) In polar regions
   D) In inland tropical areas

The correct answer is B:) Near the Tropics of Cancer and Capricorn. West coast deserts include the Atacama, Namib, and Great Sandy Deserts.

144) What is the ratio of inches to miles?

   A) 1:12
   B) 1:5405
   C) 1:36,000
   D) 1:63,360

The correct answer is D:) 1:63,360.

145) The study of landscape morphology was popularized by

   A) Thomas Malthus
   B) Carl O. Sauer
   C) Horst Graben
   D) Richard Hartshorne

The correct answer is B:) Carl O. Sauer.

146) The notion that environments determine who a person becomes is referred to as

   A) Environmental determinism
   B) Deterministic development
   C) Developmental geography
   D) Geographic determination

The correct answer is A:) Environmental determinism. This theory was reject by the geographer Carl O. Sauer in favor of the historical perspective on landscapes.

147) The author of The Nature of Geography is

    A) Thomas Malthus
    B) Carl O. Sauer
    C) Horst Graben
    D) Richard Hartshorne

The correct answer is D:) Richard Hartshorne.

148) Richard Hartshorne pulled much of his theory from _____ geographers.

    A) American
    B) French
    C) German
    D) Lithuanian

The correct answer is C:) German. Hartshorne argued that the study of geography should be limited to a purely spatial perspective, rather than incorporating various other elements.

149) At which stage of the demographic transition model would a society have high birth rates and death rates?

    A) Stage One
    B) Stage Two
    C) Stage Three
    D) Stage Four

The correct answer is A:) Stage One. The high birth and death rates characterize pre-industrial societies which are held at lower populations by their high birth and death rates.

150) Societies in Stage Three of the demographic transition model are characterized by

    A) High death rates, high birth rates
    B) Low death rates, high birth rates
    C) Low death rates, declining birth rates
    D) Low death rates, low birth rates

The correct answer is C:) Low death rates, declining birth rates. This allows a slowing of population growth and stabilizing of the society.

151) On average, the energy consumption in developed regions is _____ times greater than consumption in undeveloped regions.

    A) 100
    B) 50
    C) 10
    D) 2

The correct answer is C:) 10. For this reason, energy use is a common measure of economic development.

152) A country which has an average energy consumption of 58 watts per person would be considered

    A) Highly developed
    B) Moderately developed
    C) Average development
    D) Undeveloped

The correct answer is D:) Undeveloped. The world average for energy consumption is 300 watts.

153) Kettle and kame topography emerges as a result of

    A) Retreating glaciers
    B) Rainshadow
    C) Trade winds running parallel to a coast
    D) Uneven fault lines

The correct answer is A:) Retreating glaciers. Kettles and kames are two different and distinct land formations which are created in areas with retreating glaciers.

154) A kame is a

    A) Depression or lake formed by isolated chunks left behind when a glacier melts.
    B) Small urban center early in the urbanization process.
    C) Fault block which creates uneven terrain.
    D) Hill constructed of sediments deposited in glacial holes.

The correct answer is D:) Hill constructed of sediments deposited in glacial holes. Kettles, also formed by retreating glaciers, are described by answer A.

155) Which of the following is NOT a topographical feature found near glaciers?

    A) Kettle
    B) Karst
    C) Kane
    D) Outwash plain

The correct answer is B:) Karst. Kettles, kames, and outwash plains are all found near retreating (melting) glaciers.

156) An alluvial fan is NOT

    A) A fan-shaped mound
    B) Found near glaciers
    C) Similar to a horst
    D) All of the above are true

The correct answer is C:) Similar to a horst. A horst is an elevated area that occurs when two faults run parallel to each other.

157) Horsts and grabens are caused by

    A) Retreating glaciers
    B) Parallel running fault lines
    C) Migrating glaciers
    D) Intersecting perpendicular fault lines

The correct answer is B:) Parallel running fault lines. The parallel fault lines result in elevated and/or depressed blocks of land.

158) A graben is

    A) A pond/lake resulting from isolated chunks of unmelted glacier.
    B) A depression bounded by two normal fault lines.
    C) A hill constructed of sediments deposited by retreating glaciers.
    D) A projection bounded by two normal fault lines.

The correct answer is B:) A depression bounded by two normal fault lines. Grabens are also called rift valleys.

159) Sinkholes occur in areas with

A) Karsts
B) Grabens
C) Horst
D) Kettle

The correct answer is A:) Karsts. Karsts occur as underground water wears away at rocks, forming numerous underground caverns and fissures.

160) Which of the following is NOT a common feature of an area with karsts?

A) Sinkholes
B) Contaminated water
C) Mountains
D) Underground caverns

The correct answer is C:) Mountains. Karst regions are characterized by underground caverns, fissures, and streams, with the land above characterized by contamination of groundwater, unpredictable water supply, and sinkholes.

161) Urban populations in the United States are around

A) 10 percent
B) 30 percent
C) 50 percent
D) 80 percent

The correct answer is D:) 80 percent. Worldwide the urban populations are around 50 percent.

162) Which of the following is NOT a proper usage of the word endemic?

A) Malaria is endemic in African populations.
B) The endemic of the black plague in the 15th century was devastating to European populations.
C) The endemic cholera in less developed regions of the world is a major concern for the UN.
D) Both B and C are incorrect uses of endemic.

The correct answer is B:) The endemic of the black plague in the 15th century was devastating to European populations. The black plague would more correctly be called an epidemic.

163) How many feet are in a mile?

    A) 5280
    B) 2850
    C) 8520
    D) 8250

The correct answer is A:) 5280.

164) The presence of the Basque people in Spain is an example of a

    A) Nationalizing force
    B) Centripetal force
    C) Urbanizing force
    D) Centrifugal force

The correct answer is D:) Centrifugal force. The Basque people have remained distinct from the rest of the Spanish population due to their unique language and a fair amount of geographic isolation.

165) The belief that economic growth depends on the ability to expand and access more resources is referred to as

    A) Globalization
    B) Expansionism
    C) Imperialism
    D) Colonialism

The correct answer is B:) Expansionism. This idea became increasingly popular around the time of World Wars I and II.

166) The area with the highest population density in North American cities is

    A) At the center of the urban area
    B) A ring around the CBD
    C) A wedge moving out from the CBD
    D) On the outskirts

The correct answer is B:) A ring around the CBD. This is because people want to have as much access as possible to the commodities found in the CBD.

167) A region in which many large cities have grown together into a single large urban center is a

    A) Metropolis
    B) Necropolis
    C) Megalopolis
    D) Polygopolis

The correct answer is C:) Megalopolis. A metropolis is a large city and the suburban areas surrounding it.

 *Test Taking Strategies*

Here are some test-taking strategies that are specific to this test and to other DSST tests in general:

- Keep your eyes on the time. Pay attention to how much time you have left.

- Read the entire question and read all the answers. Many questions are not as hard to answer as they may seem. Sometimes, a difficult sounding question really only is asking you how to read an accompanying chart. Chart and graph questions are on most DANTES/DSST tests and should be an easy free point.

- If you don't know the answer immediately, the new computer-based testing lets you mark questions and come back to them later if you have time.

- Read the wording carefully. Some words can give you hints to the right answer. There are no exceptions to an answer when there are words in the question such as always, all or none. If one of the answer choices includes most or some of the right answers, but not all, then that is not the answer. Here is an example:

    The primary colors include all of the following:
        A) Red, Yellow, Blue, Green
        B) Red, Green, Yellow
        C) Red, Orange, Yellow
        D) Red, Yellow, Blue

Although item A includes all the right answers, it also includes an incorrect answer, making it incorrect. If you didn't read it carefully, were in a hurry, or didn't know the material well, you might fall for this.

- Make a guess on a question that you do not know the answer to. There is no penalty for an incorrect answer. Eliminate the answer choices that you know are incorrect. For example, this will let your guess be a 1 in 3 chance instead.

Legal Note

DSST is a registered trademark of The Thomson Corporation and its affiliated companies, and does not endorse this book.

FLASHCARDS

This section contains flashcards for you to use to further your understanding of the material and test yourself on important concepts, names or dates. Read the term or question then flip the page over to check the answer on the back. Keep in mind that this information may not be covered in the text of the study guide. Take your time to study the flashcards, you will need to know and understand these concepts to pass the test.

Ring of Fire	**Gerrymandering**
Cradle of the human race	**Confucianism originated in what country?**
Primary religion of India	**Who developed World Systems Theory?**
Buddhism originated in what country?	**Christaller's Central Place Theory uses this shape**

An attempt to establish a political advantage for a particular candidate or individual by drawing voting districts to be most advantageous

String of volcanoes

China

Africa

Wallerstein

Hinduism

Hexagon

India

CBD

Urban sprawl

LDC

HDI

Contagious diffusion

Imperialism

When water heats and condenses to water vapor it creates a

Endemic

Uncontrolled and unplanned
outward spreading of a city

Central Business District

Human Development Index

Less Developed Country

When one country takes
control of another country that
it is not adjacent to

Rapid, widespread diffusion
of a characteristic throughout
a population

A condition that is found in
a specific geographic region
and is recurring

Hurricane

Epidemic	**Universalizing religion**
Pull factors	**Doubling time**
Non-renewable resource	**Urban Heat Island**
Megalopolis	**MDC**

Has the goal of spreading throughout the world

A disease that spreads over a large space is a relatively rapid manner

The amount of time it takes for a population to double

Elements which motivate a person to want to be in another area

A hot spot on the surface of the earth that is caused by urbanization

A natural resource which cannot be generated indefinitely or sustainably

More Developed Country

Two or more metropolitan areas that are near each other and both grow to the extent that their boundaries overlap

Relocation diffusion	**Hierarchical diffusion**
Contagious diffusion	**Warren Thompson**
The Morphology of a Landscape	**The Nature of Geography**
Colonialism	**Best shape for a country**

Occurs through the individuals of authority in a culture or population	When things spread through the physical movement of individuals
Demographic transition model	A rapid, widespread diffusion of a characteristic throughout a population
Richard Hartshorne	Carl O. Sauer
Round	A particular country settles in another land and thereby gains control over it

Primate city	**John Friedman**
Core countries	**Walter Christaller**
Latitude	**Longitude**
Tropic of Cancer	**Burkina Faso is located on what continent?**

Model of Regional Development	A city that is twice the size of the next largest city in a nation
Central Place Theory	Europe, the United States, Canada, Australia, Japan, and Israel
East or West of the Equator	North or South of the Equator
Africa	25 degrees north of the equator

Isotherm lines

Metropolis

Plateaus

Maritime locations have

Aridisol

Tundras

Savannas

Most common form of cave

Large city

Outline points of equal
temperatures

More consistent temperatures

Level areas with fairly high
elevations

Cold deserts

Soil that is arid, dry, and not
suitable for the growth of
vegetation

Limestone

Transition area between
deserts and tropical
rainforests

Lightning Source UK Ltd.
Milton Keynes UK
UKHW050642240520
363416UK00018BA/578